Everything a brand does is branding

*This book is dedicated to my wife Caroline
and our two sons, Jonathan and Christopher,
who have actively, stoically and lovingly participated
in all my brand adventures.*

A BRAND IS AN ONION

Art Direction and Graphic Design by
AXEL VAGNARD

A BRAND IS AN ONION

Hugh Wilson

Why write "A Brand is an Onion"?

Good advice is arguably what people want most.
Advice from parents, tutors, friends, colleagues, mentors,
anonymous meetings and readings creates
a corpus of stimulating thoughts for each and every
one of us. The Bible puts this somewhat more succinctly:
"Wisdom crieth without".

My experience in branding, including consultancy
and teaching, has convinced me that transmitting
hard-earned knowledge in an attractive and light-
hearted fashion can stimulate other people's thinking.

Moreover I believe, as Socrates wrote, that *" I cannot
teach anybody anything. I can only make them think."*
And, if I am to believe both Montaigne and the
twentieth-century French philosopher Alain:
" one can only ever talk of one's own life."

This book is therefore an attempt to plant seeds
and light fires. My sole aim is – hopefully - to stimulate
thoughts for better branding.

Henry James described the mysterious key to
the plot of a book as *" The Figure in the Carpet "*.
If *A Brand is an Onion* is non-fiction and therefore
without a plot or figure in the carpet, the order
and structure is deliberately loose and flexible like
the file cards it stems from. The idea being for each
reader to discover the ideas that touch them most.

For those looking for a proverbial red thread,
a short handwritten sentence at the end of each chapter
summarises my thoughts on each subject.

INTRODUCTION

PANNING FOR GOLD
WE ARE WHAT WE REPEATEDLY DO

There are two golden threads that I have assiduously plaited together in Paris for over thirty years.

> The first is to have continually worked in, on, for, with and around brands and branding. *[See the timeline below]*

> The second is to have, on a daily basis, collected and curated thoughts related to branding in the broadest sense.

I came from England to France, aged twenty, to then study and work in the French luxury industry.

- ◆ Marlborough College
- ◆ La Sorbonne
- ◆ The Institute of Political Science Paris

The advantage of being " *Frenglish* " is to be able to share with an english-speaking audience some of the lessons learned when living and working with the French.

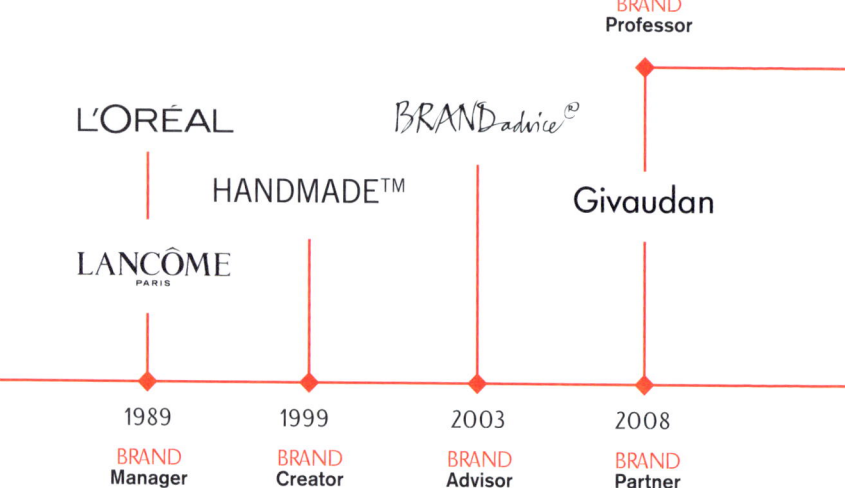

I created a brand in 1999 called HANDMADE™ that made and sold Fine English Finger Food. The colette concept store was one of my major patrons. But that was twenty years before finger food became trendy. This entrepreneurial adventure has however given me an interesting experience to share as an illustration and example throughout this book.

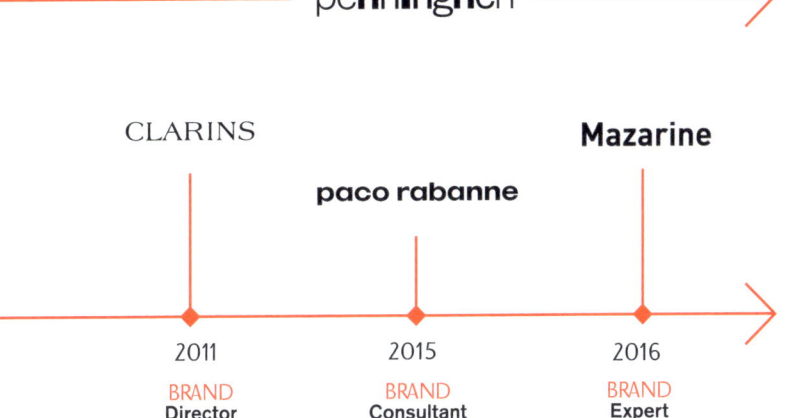

A BRAND IS AN ONION
READER'S GUIDE

THE KING OF HEARTS

I agree with the King of Hearts' first phrase in Alice in Wonderland: *"begin at the beginning"*; which is precisely what you are doing right now.

However, you can *"go on"* in any which way you please. Look at the table of contents, then dip in and out. Help yourself. Pick and choose. Or just read straight through. This is a branding manual whose practical and commonsense advice will hopefully be enlightening whatever the order of reading. It has multiple entry points and I trust will be of durable usage, time after time.

That is why I somewhat disagree with the King of Hearts when he continues, *"till you come to the end: then stop"*.

A CURIOSITY CABINET

Designed as a brand person's curiosity cabinet, A Brand is an Onion endeavors to spark thoughts and encourage discussion through geographical vibration. You are far more likely to discover an insight if you embrace an idea that you have gleaned through a surprising association, analogy, or serendipitous encounter.

The layout of this book allows your thoughts to switch from fast mode to slow, depending on the time and the place. Information, like problems, needs to be broken down into bite-sized chunks. This accounts for the block-print layout that directs, and may even improve, your concentration.

FOUR MAJOR THEMES

If this onion were to be sliced into quarters, one might reasonably discover four key themes. The chapter numbers are in brackets.

CULTURE

Style is the brand itself (5)
Culture is the future (9)
Emotions rule (11)
The fine line effect (12)
Nota bene (21)
Reading matters (33)
Quoting quotations (34)
Learning and teaching (37)
Beauty saves (38)
Gesamtkunstwerk (41)
Idiosyncrasy and genius (42)

MANAGEMENT

Perfect timing (3)
Brand memorabilia (10)
Entreprendre (13)
Favourable conditions (14)
Reality rules (15)
All work and yes play (17)
Evolving every day (18)
Management rules of thumb & managing along (19)
Yet there is method in it (26)
Public speaking (35)
Truth is beauty (39)

CREATIVITY

Serendipity (2)
Stimulating ideas (22)
Nighthinking (23)
Creative constraints (24)
Branding is about creativity (25)
On seeing and looking (27)
Flashes in fragments (28)
Picture thinking (29)
Photography brief (31)
Obsession (40)

TECHNIQUES

Colour (4)
Naming (6)
Animating promotions (7)
Digital (8)
Ordnung ist das halbe Leben (16)
For your information (20)
Short sharp simple (30)
Writing on the brand wall (32)
Attention is a chisel (36)
The difficult balance (43)

THE STRUCTURE OF EACH CHAPTER

Those who are looking for structure will be pleased to know that each chapter roughly abides by the following rules:
 I write an introduction,
and then use quotes to develop different facets of the topic.

---

10 BRAND MEMORABILIA

INTRODUCTION

Judging by the exhibitions that major luxury brands organise worldwide, you might think that part of branding is maintaining well organised archives. The saying *"if you want to know where you're going, look where you came from"* is very true. However, in general, I am dismayed at how little attention companies pay to the memory of their brand. The aforementioned luxury brands are currently investing heavily to buy back former goods and are busy creating archive museums to stock their history in ideal conditions.

Keeping daily and intelligently-pruned archives is almost a definition of brand content creation. All the drawings and photos in this book concerning HANDMADE™ obviously come from carefully organised archives.

T.S. Eliot's famous line from Four Quartets : « *time past and time future are both contained in time present* » applies perfectly to branding. <u>Brands must honour their past, embody the Zeitgest of the moment and endeavour</u> to shape the future. Easier said than done.

QUOTES

In all things, go from the known to the unknown.
Jean Guitton

Are beauty and memory separate things? Are things not beautiful because they are slightly familiar and resemble our memories?
Orhan Pamuk. Nobel Prize in literature 2006.

My one-line, handwritten, summary is to be found at the bottom of the last page of the chapter.
Any text that is not signed off with a reference is my handiwork.

> **I find going to bed and pulling my imagination over my head often means waking up with a solution to a design problem.**
>
> Alan Fletcher

Taking an hour-long photograph at night with a large format camera is both amusing and instructive. The slow-time-long-exposure allows the light-in-the-dark to gently seep in through the lens and onto the film. Is there a link between seep in and sleep in? Perhaps if one were to consider one's brain at night like the sensitive recording device it is, one might be able to develop those thought rays in the morning. No flash, just time. Night time. The brain needs time to think: load it with film early every morning and leave it on shutter release mode at night.

> **I go to sleep to come up with my ideas. I get a lot of my ideas from lucid dreaming. I've taught myself to wake up to write them down.** Daniel Lismore

> *Monks have the custom, as old as piety itself, of sowing their subject of meditation, like a seed, in the furrows of the night. They hope upon waking to find the seed already softened, penetrated by the humidity of the earth and perhaps even germinated; it will grow even more quickly in the sunbeams of reflection and grace.*
>
> **A.D. Sertillanges**

Eureka : Practice using your subconscious

CONTENTS

1	A BRAND IS AN ONION	P 18 - 29
2	SERENDIPITY	P 30 - 37
3	PERFECT TIMING	P 38 - 43
4	COLOUR	P 44 - 47
5	STYLE IS THE BRAND ITSELF	P 48 - 49
6	NAMING	P 50 - 55
7	ANIMATING PROMOTIONS	P 56 - 59
8	DIGITAL	P 60 - 63
9	CULTURE IS THE FUTURE	P 64 - 71
10	BRAND MEMORABILIA	P 72 - 75
11	EMOTIONS RULE	P 76 - 83
12	THE FINE LINE EFFECT	P 84 - 89
13	ENTREPRENDRE	P 90 - 97
14	FAVOURABLE CONDITIONS	P 98 - 103
15	REALITY RULES	P 104 - 109
16	ORDNUNG IST DAS HALBE LEBEN	P 110 - 119
17	ALL WORK AND YES PLAY	P 120 - 123
18	EVOLVING EVERYDAY	P 124 - 125
19	MANAGEMENT RULES OF THUMB & MANAGING ALONG	P 126 - 133
20	FOR YOUR INFORMATION	P 134 - 137
21	NOTA BENE	P 138 - 147
22	STIMULATING IDEAS	P 148 - 151
23	NIGHTHINKING	P 152 - 153
24	CREATIVE CONSTRAINTS	P 154 - 161

25	BRANDING IS ABOUT CREATIVITY	P 162 - 171
26	YET THERE IS METHOD IN IT	P 172 - 179
27	ON SEEING AND LOOKING	P 180 - 183
28	FLASHES IN FRAGMENTS	P 184 - 187
29	PICTURE THINKING	P 188 - 193
30	SHORT SHARP SIMPLE	P 194 - 203
31	PHOTOGRAPHY BRIEF	P 204 - 213
32	WRITING ON THE BRAND WALL	P 214 - 221
33	READING MATTERS	P 222 - 225
34	QUOTING QUOTATIONS	P 226 - 229
35	PUBLIC SPEAKING	P 230 - 233
36	ATTENTION IS A CHISEL	P 234 - 235
37	LEARNING AND TEACHING	P 236 - 241
38	BEAUTY SAVES	P 242 - 245
39	TRUTH IS BEAUTY	P 246 - 247
40	OBSESSION	P 248 - 253
41	GESAMTKUNSTWERK	P 254 - 255
42	IDIOSYNCRASY AND GENIUS	P 256 - 257
43	THE DIFFICULT BALANCE	P 258 - 263
	MY TAKE ON EACH CHAPTER	P 264 - 265
	ONION TYPE DESIGN	P 266 - 267
	NEXT STEPS	P 268 - 269
	CREDITS AND THANKS	P 270 - 273
	INDEX OF AUTHORS QUOTED	P 274 - 282
	YOUR FINDINGS	P 283 - 287

Onions are visibly coherent. From skin to core, each layer is perfectly adjusted to the next and each slice unmistakably part of the whole. Perhaps the perfect figurative model for a Brand. You can't say the same about potatoes.

1

A BRAND IS AN

1 A BRAND IS AN ONION

I firmly believe that the creator of a brand sets out to create a better world. A world that she or he would rather live in. If enough people share that vision, then the brand will prosper. Creating a brand is a labour of love. You can't become a love brand if you don't give it love. Love in; love out. People recognise themselves in your brand. They share your values. They see the work you put in. A brand is what people think and feel about it. Brands must fight to fulfil their promise, keep their oath and honour their pledge. Brands are concept-worlds created by and for bonded bands of people.

Everything a brand does is branding. That's why branding is so important in the creation of company reputation and brand equity. And that's why I like the onion metaphor : an onion looks like a planet, a spherical world, and inside it is organised with great coherency. Every part of an onion is distinctly and unmistakably "onion". Onions always keep their promise : they make you cry, but have a lovely taste. And like brands, there is very little difference between onions, but it is that little difference that makes all the difference.*

> Funnily enough, I've never seen a branded onion. Tangerines often come wrapped in individual tissue paper with a logo stuck on. But not onions. Perhaps there's a business opportunity for onion-growers here.

*[cf The Fine Line Effect chp 12]

What is a brand?

It is said that the prostitutes of Alexandria, in ancient times, chiselled their initials under the sole of their sandals in negative. Thus the potential customer on reading them printed on the sand of the beach, would recognize both the desired person and the direction of her mattress.

The CEOs of major brands advertising on our city walls will undoubtedly enjoy learning that they are the direct descendants of those aforementioned whores. Michel Serres. Philosopher.

A Brand is an ambition. A Brand is an answer. A [Brand] is an asset. A Brand is an attitude. A Brand is a [...] is a benefit. A Brand is a celebrity. A Brand is [...] Brand is a commitment. A Brand is a community[...] is confidence. A Brand is consideration. A Bran[d is conti]nuity. A Brand is a contract. A Brand is a conve[rsation.] Brand is a culture. A Brand is a desire. A Brand [is...] A Brand is an emotion. A Brand is an engager[. A Brand is] an expectation. A Brand is an experience. A B[rand is a] feeling. A Brand is a flag. A Brand is a founder. [A Brand is a] history. A Brand is holistic. A Brand is humour. [A Brand is an] ideology. A Brand is idiosyncratic. A Brand is a[...] Brand is a language. A Brand is a legacy. A Bra[nd is a way] of life. A Brand is a logo. A Brand is a love bite[. A Brand is a] meaning. A Brand is a memory. A Brand is a m[...] Brand is a movement. A Brand is a myth. A Bra[nd is...] A Brand is an onion. A Brand is an opinion. A B[rand is a] personality. A Brand is a perspective. A Brand [is a point] of view. A Brand is a position. A Brand is a pos[...] profit. A Brand is a project. A Brand is a promis[e. A Brand is a] frustration. A Brand is a religion. A Brand is a re[...] A Brand is a school. A Brand is a selfie. A Bra[nd is a] signature. A Brand is sharing. A Brand is singu[lar. A Brand] is a sound. A Brand is a souvenir. A Brand is [...] Brand is a strategy. A Brand is a symbol. A Bra[nd is...] Brand is a tattoo. A Brand is a theatre. A Brand [is a] trace. A Brand is a trail. A Brand is trustworthy[. A Brand] is a value. A Brand is a voice. A Brand is a visio[n. A Brand is more] than the sum of its parts. A brand is a why. A B[rand is...]

s an animation. A Brand is anticipation. A Brand Brand is behaviour. A Brand is a belief. A Brand tele. A Brand is a code. A Brand is a colour. A nd is a compass. A Brand is a concept. A Brand temporary. A Brand is content. A Brand is conti-. A Brand is a creation. A Brand is a crusade. A logue. A Brand is different. A Brand is a dream. Brand is equity. A Brand is ethical. A Brand is an expression. A Brand is a family. A Brand is d is a god. A Brand is a guarantee. A Brand is a is an identity. A Brand is an icon. A Brand is an e. A Brand is an invention. A Brand is a label. A legend. A Brand is a location. A Brand is a sign nd is a man. A Brand is a marker. A Brand is a . A Brand is a method. A Brand is a mission. A name. A Brand is an oath. A Brand is an offer. particular. A Brand is perseverant. A Brand is a losophy. A Brand is a pledge. A Brand is a point Brand is power. A Brand is a price. A Brand is nd is a reason to believe. A Brand is relief from n. A Brand is a relationship. A Brand is reliable. sensation. A Brand is a shortcut. A Brand is a rand is a smell. A Brand is a solution. A Brand A Brand is a statement. A Brand is a story. A system. A Brand is a style. A Brand is a taste. A ought. A Brand is a tone of voice. A Brand is a nd is a typography. A Brand is unique. A Brand and is a way of life. A Brand is a whole greater a woman. A Brand is a world. A Brand is work.

A brand is the most valuable piece of real estate in the world : a corner of someone's mind. John Hegarty

Like "Star Wars", Harry Potter is a feat of world-building, with its own laws and vocabulary that turn fans into obsessives. Emma Jacobs

> Your Brand is what other people say about you, when you´re not in the room. Jeff Bezos

> **A brand is a symbolic envelope around a person, a product, a place or a service. We create brands to add value to what we are consuming.** Delphine Dion

Beethoven is a Brand. Shakespeare and Manchester United are too. They are worlds. We tend to prefer everything that comes before us with the organic strength of a world. It is an insurance against chaos, it is an organization that safeguards reality. Alessandro Baricco

> The moment you're identified as a style, you're marketed. You have a price, a colour, a taste… I want my brand to be blurry. Eric Judor. Actor.

A Brand must deliver the promise no one else in the industry dares to make. Michael Gerber

A Brand is a posture.

Apple's former promise was that you didn't have to worry about how the device worked. The new promise is that you don't have to worry about whether their technology is ripping you off. **Benedict Evans.**

Every definition is a cage.
Christian Bobin

A lot of young people I know talk about "working on their brand", and sometimes I wish that word had never been invented. A person has a soul. A brand has a reputation. A person has private dignity. A brand is a creation for an audience. David Brooks

Id Est: Everything a brand does is branding

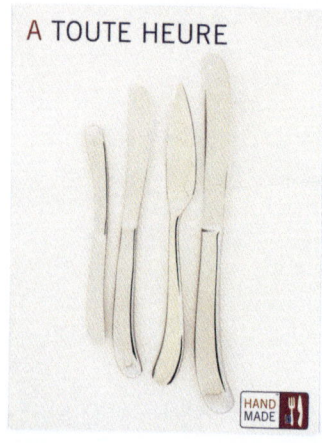

WATER L'EAU

SHORTBREAD

These 14 postcards [and posters] illustrated with Guido Mocafico's photographs hopefully sum up the spirit of HANDMADE™ : lighthearted but beautifully meaningful.

COFFEE BREAK

DEJEUNER SUR L'HERBE

GO AND EAT
EAT AND GO

BREAKFAST

2

Seren

dipity

"Accidental sagacity"

Horace Walpole. Inventor of the word serendipity.
Letter to Horace Mann. 28 january 1754.

2 SERENDIPITY. A SYNONYM FOR INNOVATION?

The internet has shone a new spotlight on the word serendipity. Algorithms dig out semi-related subjects to those you initially search.

> To me, serendipity is a way of observing the world, of systematically scanning for ideas relevant to one's life and job. Journalists who have hunches that they then follow are said to be "gathering string". Brands should behave likewise, constantly on the lookout for ideas that stimulate innovation.
> *Serendipity requires paying attention; nurturing an open and curious mind.* Newton's apple was just a trigger for a mind constantly thinking.

Every brand should create an internal stimulating-ideas-forum to foster innovation. I see the forum as a figurative pinball machine that flips ideas around the company, increasing the chances of lucky connections that might lead to new products or services.

> You can't invent ideas; you have to look for them where they are. Alain

Serendipity is more of an attitude than anything else. The more you scan the world, looking for thoughts to enrich your brand, the more interesting facts, people and ideas you find.

In reality, discoveries are not really made by chance.

Newton's apple was just a trigger for a mind constantly thinking

They are made possible because the person who makes these discoveries has put himself in a certain state of mind composed of openness, availability, curiosity, wonder, astonishment, analogical and symbolic thinking, which allows us to see what brings together rather than what divides. Christian Vanden Berghen

EXAMPLES OF SERENDIPITY

- Nylon
- Play-Doh
- Segway
- Velcro
- Dental implants
- America
- Tarte Tatin
- Bêtises de Cambrai
- Penicillin
- Microwave
- Artificial sweeterners

- Safety glass
- Photosynthesis
- Ambient music
- Viagra
- Ski jumping
- Smoke detectors
- The Scream by Munch
- Animal Farm by Orwell
- Pendulum
- Rimowa
- X-Ray
- Uber

A WALK AT THE ORIGIN OF VELCRO

In 1941, George de Mestral, a 34-year-old Swiss engineer who had just returned from hunting, wanted to remove the plants clinging to his clothes. Intrigued by the resistance of the blue Alpine thistles, he examined them under a microscope and found that they have tiny hooks that cling to the loops in the stitches of cloth, but once detached, they regain their original shape.

George de Mestral had a very inventive mind (he filed his first patent at the age of 12) and immediately imagined two strips of cotton, one with hooks, the other with loops. But it took him nearly 10 years, with the collaboration of a teacher from the Institut Textile de France, to develop the final version of the Velcro® (acronym for «velvet crochet») strips. Jacques Henno

JAN BAPTIST VAN HELMONT WEIGHS A WILLOW TREE. *Belgium, early 17th century.*

Van Helmont, a Flemish chemist, planted a seed in a pot. Five years later, the soil weighed the same – but a 75kg tree had grown out of it. Where had it come from? The answer is air, and his experiment was the start of the science of photosynthesis. *The Economist*

Scanners finders; finders keepers.
Hugh Wilson

GEORGE ORWELL THINKS LIKE A HORSE

England 1943. Out for a walk, Orwell saw a little boy whipping a carthorse, and wondered what would happen if the animal realised that it was stronger than the boy. Two years later he published "Animal Farm". *Intelligent Life*

LUCID SERENDIPITY

In June of 1833, joining friends and family on an outing to sketch the beauty of the Lake Como landscape, William Henry Fox Talbot became frustrated by his remarkable inability to draw. While the rest of the group was producing fluent recordings of the exquisite topography, his own dismal output depressed him. He later claimed that it was then that he postulated the notion of asking the scene to draw its own image on light sensitive materials. *First Photographs.* Arthur Ollman.

MUNCH
" sensed a scream passing through nature "

CULTIVATING THE ART OF SERENDIPITY

Innovation isn't all hard work or dumb luck : it's about paying attention. At its birth, serendipity meant a skill rather than a random stroke of good fortune.
> Super-encounterers reported that happy surprises popped up wherever they looked, because they counted on finding treasures in the oddest places.

"Gathering string" is an old newsroom term to describe the first stage of reporting, when you're looking for something that you can't yet name.
> String is everywhere for the taking,
> if you have the talent to take it.

As people dredge the unknown, they are engaging in a highly creative act. What an inventor "finds" is always an expression of himself or herself.

Pagan Kennedy. *International New York Times.* 2 January 2016.

The more I practice, the luckier I get.

Jerry Barber. Golfer.

Chance favours only the prepared mind.
Pasteur. Scientist.

You can find inspiration in everything *
***and if you can't, look again.**

[Title of a book] by Paul Smith

Ideas come from everything and everywhere.
David Lynch.
Film Director & Artist.

It takes a lot of searching to find chance.
Laurent Terzieff.
French actor.

The writer listens for words that shape his future.
Edmond Jabès.
French poet.

Serendipity can only take place for those who are endowed with stubbornness, sagacity and flexibility of mind.
Denis Grozdanovitch

Where is the idea?
Alain

Amazing coincidence that maps out your path.
Student at Penninghen 2009

Perchance Alert minds gather string

3 PERFECT TIMING

> Optimal – if never quite perfect – timing is an extremely important yet often underestimated lesson in branding.

Perfect timing is most often seen in sport. A half volley in cricket, a pass in rugby, a tackle in football. Apparently the famous Italian football defender Paolo Maldini timed his positioning so well that he only had to make an average of 1.8 tackles per match.

> In the 1960's my mother was undoubtedly right to pick up litter on the beach and in the 1990s me riding a bicycle to work in Paris was both good for my health and for the planet. But it was not the done thing at the time. The time was not ripe.

I was once Marketing Director at Givaudan, the world leader in the creation of fragrances. Part of my job was to advise Brand Managers from fine fragrance brands on what kind of perfume to launch. I would cover all angles, from naming to bottle design to the fragrance itself, but I would always conclude with a caveat: the most important aspect, perfect timing, is always out of your control. Givaudan happened to have created the fragrance One Million for Paco Rabanne, whose blockbuster success was seen as brilliant timing.

> The truth is that it was just good luck. It takes years to develop such a project. And obviously nobody knew in advance that the launch of a virile scent, in a somewhat tacky - but well made - imitation

gold bullion bottle, would be perceived as tongue-in-cheek light relief from the Financial Crisis of 2008.

The popular business motto is to be in the right place at the right time - with the right product. Calvin, the brat with the tiger Hobbes in Bill Watterson's brilliant comic strip, probably voices the truth when he quips: " since you never know when the right time is going to be, I figure the trick is to find the right place and just hang around ". Interestingly enough, Nestlé's Nespresso concept was launched in 1986, but only blossomed in 2006...

It's not a question *of this being right*, it's just a question *of when it's right.*

Jonathan Ive. Apple.

Social media has recently brought precise timing to the fore. What is the ideal time of the day to post on Instagram?

Clinical studies have recently shown that the efficiency of cancer treatments can increase five-fold if administered at the optimal moment in the patient's biological cycle.

The art of timing in branding is definitely a skill to be honed. The Ancient Greeks knew that centuries ago. They had a god called Kairos, who had very long hair so you could easily seize him by the mane when he passed by!

THERE IS NO *RIGHT TIME*

READ

Time is the reward for fame. I write by hand to slow the process down. Above all, I lie to my editor. I always tell him I'm not finished, otherwise he'll put pressure on me, tell me it's the "right time" to release it. I don't care about the "right time". There is no "right time". Just a good novel.
John Irving. American Author.

Christopher Lloyd, one of England's most famous gardeners was always being asked : "when should I prune this, when should I plant that?". Towards the end of his life, his laconic reply was: "when you're in the mood !"

ZEITGEIST IN A BOTTLE: **Sniffing the spirit of the times, capturing its essence and restoring it in its slightest notes, to the point of being able to bring back a precise moment of our life in all its strength... such is the work of *mythical perfumes*.** Marie Bénédicte Gauthier. *Parfums mythiques.*

Nothing stops an idea whose time has come.   Victor Hugo

NESS IS ALL

To be right too early is to be wrong.
Hugh Wilson

An artist's duty is to reflect the times.
Nina Simone

The people who rush in first fail; the companies that come up behind end up winners.
Richard Waters

William Shakespeare

An algorithm can tell if a tweet came from a human, a robot or a marketing mailout. The key factor? Timing.

There's nothing in this world that doesn't have a decisive moment.

Cardinal de Retz. 1613-1679. French statesman & author.
Quoted by Henri Cartier Bresson in his famous 1952 text:
"The decisive instant".

Optimal timing
Just-in-time
The decisive moment
Ideal timing
Favourable timing
The time *is ripe*
Timing *is paramount*
Timing *is all*
A keen sense of timing
Timing *is crucial*

TIMING IS MONEY

In 1998, the French press was full of optimistic signs concerning the development of the fast food market. A year later, after opening my upmarket finger food concept HANDMADE™ I learnt, *at my expense*, that habits in general and eating habits in particular take a very long time to change.

Another lesson was that French scorn concerning English food will probably never change, however many million sandwiches Marks & Spencer may have sold since they arrived in Paris in the 1980s. Even very recently, when writing about Brexit, the French business newspaper *Les Echos* wrote: " one can never trust British cooks ! "

And it is not because journalists or leaders of opinion like your concept that the public will necessarily buy into it straightaway. Timing is everything.

When ? Kairos is a powerful lever to success

4 COLOUR

FERRARIS are always red, unless they're yellow.
ASTON MARTINS are best in silver. TIFFANY made turquoise chic. CHANEL seems to own the colour black* and its success in establishing black as the colour of luxury has tempted many well established cosmetic brands to abandon their historic colours, just to follow suit. But as colour is itself a marker of distinction, this copycat approach to luxury is hardly intelligent branding. One only has to mention the brand names: Coca-Cola, Hermès, Selfridges, Carlsberg, Facebook, Cadbury and Silk Cut to see rainbow " Richard Of York Gained Battle In Vain " mnenomics appear.

> Fluorescent colours made a bad name for themselves through discount price signs, but when used in different circumstances fluorescent reds, oranges and yellows can be extremely distinctive and amusing.
> Selfridges knows that. Illuminated manuscripts always used the most striking of colours. Burnished gold catches light beautifully, not to mention the splendid pinks and blues used by medieval scribes.

If there are only seven colours in the rainbow, the human eye can apparently distinguish 10 million different colours, which leaves room for brands to pick and choose. Especially if they combine several. Talking of combining colours, it was only when printing colour cards for a Lancôme make-up brochure that I was told that four-colour printing can in fact be as-many-colours-as-you-can-afford printing. In this particular case we ended up using twelve, enabling violets and mauves to at last become wonderfully luminous.

*Purists might object that black is not a colour per se, but a shade; as in darkest shades of grey or a blacker shade of pale... Black is actually a very difficult colour to obtain. The artists Gilbert & George have worked on the subject almost all their lives and recently Anish Kapoor, to the dismay of the art world, controversially bought the patent to Vantablack, a 99.96% blackest of blacks.

This is not a book on colours. But brands-to-be should carefully consider the symbolic meanings of colour that can change depending on geography, culture and religion.

CAN A COLOUR BELONG TO A BRAND?

In 2004, Cadbury launched a process to register the Pantone 2685C purple shade used on the packaging of its chocolate products. Nestlé succeeded in having this trademark registration annulled by the Court of Appeal.

TIFFANY BLUE

It's the only brand in the world that owns a colour.

Bernard Arnault. *Les Echos*. 26 Novembre 2019.

FERRARIS
are always red,

unless they're
yellow.

HANDMADE™
Systematically used its two brand colours (Blue and Red) on all written documents. Red is a colour that naturally stands out, so was reserved for highlighting important words.

Perhaps the overall aspect harks back to my childhood, where the pupil's handwriting in blue ink would be interspersed with the teacher's corrections in red.

I often feel that Brands could use typography to better display their corporate colours.

As they say, writing is you on paper.

Autrement dit: Don't underestimate the power of colour

5 STYLE
IS THE BRAND ITSELF

My first notable encounter with style was when studying modern history at the Institute of Political Science in Paris. I noticed the clear difference in literary style between Winston Churchill and Charles de Gaulle. Whereas the English call a spade a spade, the French call a cat a cat. The French word " chat " [cat] is decidedly softer, more feminine and refined than the direct and more practical English word "spade " . To make a preposterously broad generalisation ; Churchill uses plain words, where De Gaulle uses elegant ones. English versus French. Bulldog versus Cock. Pragmatism versus Sophistication. Perhaps truth versus beauty, which combine, or crunch - at Twickenham, in the words of John Keats to form " *beauty is truth, truth beauty* " . These national traits may be oversimplified, but both countries have their soft power skills and their style. And so do Brands. *Ã chaque marque son style.*

Style is the man himself; style cannot be stolen, transported, or altered; if it is elevated, noble and sublime, the author will be admired equally in all times, for only truth is durable and everlasting.
Buffon. French naturalist and author. 1753.

> Style is the thought itself.
> — Joseph Joubert

> Proper words in proper places make the true definition of style.
> — Jonathan Swift

> Style is the shape of meaning.
> — Paul Valéry

> The idea gives the style.
> — Alain

> Style is the inflection imparted to ideas by material conditions.
> — Alain

> Fashion fades, style remains.
> — Coco Chanel

> Style is only the order and movement you put into your thoughts.
> — Buffon

> God has no style.
> — Picasso

> Style: a way for everyone to be identical to themselves, everywhere.
> — Christian Bobin

> Metaphors alone give a kind of eternity to style.
> — Marcel Proust

In a word: Manners maketh brands

6 NAMING

> One of the most important acts in branding is naming. A name immediately conjures up an emotion in people's minds.

Depending on their culture, personal history and language: people's reaction can be very different from what one might initially think. I soon discovered that the name HANDMADE™, whilst very understandable when written, would – more often than not – be pronounced "Mohammed" by the French. My accountant never quite got his tongue around my brand's name.

> Even if today, on Amazon, many Chinese brands selling generic products seem to manage to get away with stringing random letters together, the name of a brand remains a fundamental act. A brand's name, however old and famous the brand, continues to be important, as The Royal Bank of Scotland crisis proves, three centuries after its birth.

The choice of the word "HANDMADE™" for my brand was an attempt to name, describe and explain in one fell swoop. A desire to call a spade a spade. If the word is indeed generic, it was not considered as such by the French patent officials, for whom it was a foreign word and therefore perfectly acceptable as a novel brand name on French soil.

My plan was to start off in France and pivot later if the name caused a problem when going international.

After all, I thought, the former national French Telecom company had changed its name to *Orange* which is equally as generic as *Handmade*. There seems to be a small loophole here. The only other two names I have ever registered were also English word combinations that went unhindered through the red tape here in France: **Picture-Thinking©** and **BrandAdvice®**.

OLD	NEW
Google Inc	**Alphabet**
Snapchat	**Snap**
France Télécom	**Orange**
PPR	**Kering**
Holland	**Netherlands**
Yves Saint Laurent	**Saint Laurent**
Covoiturage	**BlaBlaCar**
SeeConcept	**Izipizi**
Geely	**Link & Co**

Christopher ? John ? François ?

The name of a company defines its identity. For the company VTC Kapten, formerly Chauffeur Privé, the change of name was the condition for its entry into on the London market, otherwise no one would have been able to pronounce its name.
This put 250 employees to work for three months and increased the marketing budget fivefold. The name *Kapten* also changed the up-market connotation of *Chauffeur Privé*.

Gaëlle Caradec. *Les Echos.* 1 Octobre 2019

We are subject to social structuring the minute we are born, because of the simple choice others have made in giving us our first name. Journal of Personality & Social Psychology. *Le Monde.* 15 March 2017.

WE AND US. FROM A TO Z.

I didn't want to call it Alber Elbaz, because it's not about me, myself and I. It's going to be about we and us. And it's going to go from A to Z. It's going to be about things I believe are relevant to make. Alber Elbaz, AZfashion.

To name things wrongly is to add to the misfortune of this world.
Albert Camus

NAMING *IS CREATING* To name something is not simply to say or reflect on what is. It is also to create, to bring into existence. The word itself has the power to forge a world, to magnetize forces or disperse them. Ideas or behaviours that until then were imperceptible or almost non-existent can, through a name, come to life.
Roger-Pol Droit. Philosopher.

> Have you noticed? The tech giants are calling their intelligent assistants by human names: Alexa, Watson, Albert...
> This terminology is intended in particular to reassure a general public that is sometimes circumspect about Artificial Intelligence. And it helps to create an emotional bond.
> *Les Echos Week-End.* 13 Juillet 2017.

A name and also an omen

NOMEN ATQUE OMEN

Plautus (254-184 B.C.)

In 1971, Bernard Arnault visited the US for the first time. He asked a New York taxi driver what he knew of France. "*He could not name the president but he knew Dior*", he often recounts. Harriet Agnew. *The Financial Times*. 22nd June 2019.

HELVETICA: YOU LOOK LIKE YOUR NAME

Neue Haas Grotesk was soon renamed Helvetica under pressure from the majority shareholder of the Haas foundry, who wanted to capitalize on Switzerland's reputation in this sector. «*Our product was sold as an embodiment of the national spirit: modesty, simplicity, timelessness*».

Alfred Hoffmann-Feet,
92 years old, son of the owner of the Haas foundry.

Pour info: Names shape behaviour

7 ANIMATING PROMOTIONS

I created the marketing animation department at Lancôme International in 1994. That meant that for the first time ever, all the Lancôme subsidiaries worldwide would, theoretically, have to " buy " their animations and promotions from headquarters in Paris. To take the only creative marketing activity away from the local applied marketing teams meant learning from and with them, in order to gradually provide acceptable, and hopefully superior, propositions.

Here below are the lessons I learnt from that four-year experience, put into simple rules that apply whatever the subject.

> **Literally speaking, the word animate means to give life, to breathe life into something. Synonyms are:**
> *to excite, to agitate, to sharpen.*

The famous, and now regrettably closed, Parisian concept store " Colette ", with whom HANDMADE™ partnered, was the epitome of brand animation in action (*even if Colette and Sarah would refuse to acknowledge that they had become a brand!*). I would often drive past on a Sunday evening, only to see Colette herself busy installing the window display for the coming week. Colette's whole concept was about breathing life into shopping, creating novelty on a permanent basis. Her first - *and perhaps most memorable* - animation was to create a " water bar ", where a different water bottle manufacturer was put on animation every week. Theatre it was indeed. The extraordinary glorifying of the ordinary.

THE SUBJECT IS THE STORY

The story of an animation is the theme (Christmas, Saint Valentine's Day, Summer...) multiplied by your brand.

STORY = THEME x BRAND

I thought the student who chose Bic ballpoint pens answered the equation " Subject x Brand " pretty perfectly.

It's not *what* you say, it's *how you* say it!

An animation should be banal, but singular; expected, but unexpected.

Everything depends on the way things are done, on the manner in which the animation is designed and produced.

The **THREE THUMB RULES** that seem to work, whatever the subject – and I have tested this theory on at least 30 different animations – are as follows:

1. AN ATYPICAL COLOUR. At Lancôme, we once created a Summer animation using fluorescent orange. This is obviously slightly more expensive to produce than a classical quadrichromy print, but it undoubtedly persuaded Les Galeries Lafayette to give us ten consecutive windows on the Boulevard Haussman. You might call this the Andy Warhol rule: Marylin Monroe in a variety of atypical colours being a good example.

2. REMARKABLE GRAPHICS. By remarkable, I mean graphics that the eye remarks. The Nike swoosh is, graphically speaking, more remarkable than a circle. The Union Jack is – to judge from the number of articles of clothing it adorns – more remarkable than national flags that fly three different bands of colour.

3. A SIMPLE THEME. Animation themes are often what the French amusingly call " cream pies " [tartes à la crème] because they are worn out commonplace clichés. Christmas, or Chinese New Year, are cream pies in point. These themes come round every twelve months on the very same day and require novel angles, both for the theme itself and the brand in question. My recommendation is to keep the theme as clear and as understandable as possible. The manner in which each brand tackles the subject, in its own idiosyncratic way, being the key to originality.

Verdict : *Vitality is a virtue*

8 DIGITAL   B.C. / DIGITAL / A.D.

This tongue in cheek reference to a watershed
year for Christians has its serious side. " B.efore
C.omputers and A.fter D.igital " does mark
a distinct period in history. My belief is that
we should try and keep alive certain habits
and knowledge from the analogue pre-computer
world. I consider myself lucky to be part of what
one might call "*The Bridge Generation*",
those analogue-natives who have become digital-
learners. I even encourage digital-natives to become
analogue-learners. My fourth year Art Students
are systematically astounded
at the enjoyment they procure from taking
a photograph using a large-format analogue
camera on a tripod. They are amazed at
the size of the removable lens, astounded with
the beauty of the live, reversed and upside down
image on the ground glass. Not to mention
the quality and beauty of the final object,
that they have to wait until the next lesson to see.

Digital is with us to stay. It is absolutely fantastic
in many respects and just needs to be contemplated
with a little common sense. " Safety first "
[or perhaps " Save first "] is probably an advisable
rule of thumb in the binary online world, whilst
maintaining the best of what the " real world "
has to offer too.

It is ironic that screens - *which etymologically signify obstacles -* have become the main mediator between human beings and the favoured access to our surroundings. Marianne Durano

> **Once your cucumber brain has become pickled, it can never go back to being a cucumber.**
> *The Financial Times*

> Today's dungeons are called «screens».
> They're worse than the walls of a cell.
> They go up everywhere. You can't see them
> and you can't knock them down. Sylvain Tesson

Google can bring you 100,000 answers but a librarian can bring you the right one. Mahesh Rao

> Black Mirror assumes that people – enough people anyway – will look at any new device the way a terrorist looks at a truck or a boxcutter, with an eye toward the damage they can do with it.
> *The New York Times.* 4 January 2018.

When Microsoft closes its e-book store later this month, every novel, biography, self-help guide and history book will cease to work. These stories of vanishing books reveal the unpleasant reality behind the convenience of online purchases. Microsoft is offering full refunds, plus $25 for users who have annotated their copies. A book in hand could well be worth two on an e-reader. *The Financial Times.* **6th July 2019.**

> Backup systems change faster, alas, than a mortal's heart. *Hence the importance of handwritten notes.* Jakuta Alikavavazovic

*Tools are not neutral,
they shape the person who handles them.*

Marianne Durano

What I need to know *is not* on Google.

Sam Shepard

I miss my pre-internet brain.

Douglas Coupland

If you want to do a sketch, *no software beats a pen and paper.*

India Knight

There's no way to shove genies back into bottles.

Nilanjana Roy

The CIA can listen to your phone, even if you turn it off.

Les Echos

You still need your brain.

Daniel T Willingham

THE CHOICE WE FACE isn't between *digital* and *analogue*.

The real world isn't black or white. It's not even grey.

Reality is multi-coloured, infinitely textured & emotionally layered.

David Sax

B.C./A.D. All is not digital. Stand on the bridge

9 CULTURE IS *THE FUTURE*

Culture and general knowledge are both sources of joy as well as being the essential tools of branding. General knowledge is similar to common sense, in that it requires an open, curious mind like that of a child.

I read recently that children ask up to 40,000 questions before they are six. That's about 20 questions a day! General knowledge is the outcome of maintaining a similar, inquisitive attitude throughout life.

I agree with Hegel who said that reading a daily newspaper is the modern man's equivalent to religion. I was once in Marrakech and had to go on a long trek across town to buy *Le Monde*. Upon my return, my host quipped that " the only thing that changes in a newspaper is the date ". There may have been a soupçon of truth in that remark, especially as the French press arrives a day late in Morocco. My Moroccan friend echoes Proust's comment in *Swann's Way*, that newspapers are full of insignificant things and that we should read proper books instead. Flaubert was probably closer to the truth when he complained, that one cannot do without newspapers, but that one should " thunder against them"! It is however rare that I cannot find some new and interesting thought on a daily basis. You never quite know what nugget you will find. It's like panning for gold.

**He who knows only his generation
always remains a child.** Cicero

With practice you learn to sift the chaff from the wheat fairly fast. And if you diligently collect these pearls of wisdom, in time they become what one might also call general knowledge. I know Google's unfathomable knowledge is great, but it is their encyclopedia, not yours.

General knowledge is what General Managers need most. The first time I was about to interview an intern for L'Oréal, my boss told me only to consider whether the young graduate in question might, a few decades later, be able to become General Manager of the Group. The only way you can begin to answer that conundrum is to try and establish whether the candidate has an open and curious mind: culture being what makes the future.

Knowledge is knowing how to act.
Henri Bergson. Philosopher.

**Culture is the most important thing.
That's what brings joy to life,
it's the value of living.**
Hans Rosling

Knowledge itself is power.
Francis Bacon. Philosopher.

I like to know everything.
I am a sort of universal concierge,
not an intellectual.
Karl Lagerfeld

*Sapience is neither knowledge, nor wisdom,
but the knowledge that leads to wisdom.*
Eugène Green. Film maker.

> General culture should be considered as a propensity to curiosity, not as a sum of knowledge, and must become a priority for all businesses.
>
> **Olivier Babeau. Sapiens Institute.**

The farther back you can look, the farther forward you are likely to see. ♦ Winston Churchill

> *Your home is your culture; it's not the ground you live on, it's the belief system you carry with you.*
>
> **Rufus Norris. Theatre Director.**

General knowledge is measuring the extent of one's ignorance.

Pierre-Henri Tavoillot. Philosopher.

Culture is neither a luxury nor food for the soul; it is the only reasonable safeguard against dehumanisation caused by uncontrolled globalisation. Martine Robert

General Knowledge is knowing 100 words more than other people.
Frédéric Dard

There has been a paradigm shift from the search for experiences to reach for something beyond – an accumulation of knowledge, if you like. The very rich, when they travel, want to understand, to learn, to reflect on history and to gain an insight into other cultures. Adrien Chang.
CEO K11 Musea Concept Hong Kong.

Culture is the memory of a perfume in an empty bottle. Jean Guitton. Philosopher.

The transmission of our inventions, discoveries and creations – technical, scientific, artistic… – is our only bulwark against death and nothingness.
Roger-Pol Droit. Philosopher.

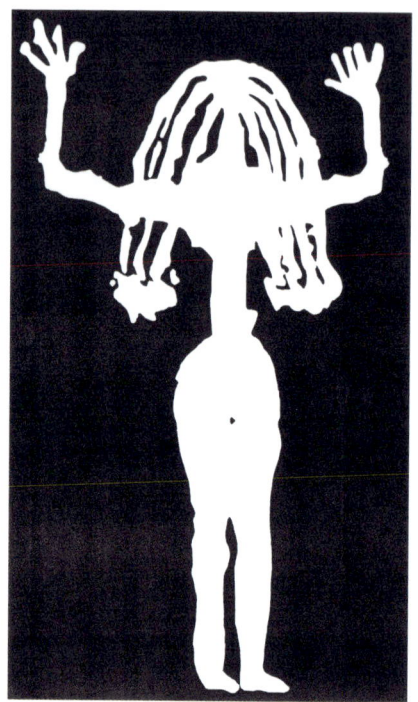

CULTURE AS ADDED VALUE

Children eating cereals alone in the morning spend hours, half-awake, reading and re-reading the marketing blurb on the back of cereal boxes. If only, I have always thought, that quiet captive time were spent reading something more interesting. Just as French women always take a book to the beach, in order to avoid " idiot tanning " as the popular French expression goes, when I created HANDMADE™ we provided lone gourmets with bespoke intellectual games to offer "intelligent eating". (See overleaf) This was all part of my desire to create as much " Value Added Culture" as possible. The stone shelves, for example, were installed Donald Judd style, the honey-coloured flagstones were cut and laid as if they were wooden floorboards and the graphic style of the logo was based on a cave painting. (See opposite) Every effort was made to give meaning or to add what Proust called " thicknesses of art " .

Proust describes culture as added value in *Swann's Way*.
" The truth was that she could never make up her mind to purchase anything from which no intellectual profit was to be derived. She attempted by a subterfuge, if not to eliminate altogether their commercial banality, at least to minimise it, to substitute for the bulk of it what was art still, to introduce, as it might be, several 'thicknesses' of art; instead of photographs of Chartres Cathedral, of the Fountains of Saint-Cloud, or of Vesuvius she would inquire of Swann whether some great painter had not made pictures of them, and preferred to give me photographs of 'Chartres Cathedral' after Corot, of the 'Fountains of Saint-Cloud' after Hubert Robert, and of 'Vesuvius' after Turner, which were a stage higher in the scale of art."

Fundamental: Culture gives and makes sense

Frequently Asked Questions

ANACHRONISMES LA TROISIÈME RÉPUBLIQUE

Un jeu de culture générale au sens propre. Regarder une époque de façon générale et transversale afin de créer des liens entre les disciplines.Le but du jeu : repérer le personnage, fait ou objet qui ne fait pas partie de l'époque évoquée. C'est-à-dire chercher l'anachronisme.

1.POLITIQUE Entente Cordiale
2.ÉCONOMIE Percement du canal de Suez
3.BEAUX-ARTS Rodin
4.LITTÉRATURE Maupassant
5.ARCHITECTURE Hector Guimard
6.DÉCORATION William Morris
7.DÉCOUVERTE Le téléphone
8.MUSIQUE Debussy

HAND MADE

La Troisième République remplace l'Empire de Napoléon III et durera jusqu'à la Première Guerre Mondiale (1870 - 1914).
1. Entente Cordiale (1904). Accord colonial franco-anglais, début d'un rapprochement. Edouard VII et Paul Cambon en furent les artisans. 2. Percement du canal de Suez. Anachronisme (d'un an). Ferdinand de Lesseps commença les travaux en 1859. Le canal fut inauguré en 1869. 3. Rodin (1840 - 1917). Sculpteur très indépendant, il est difficile d'inscrire son oeuvre dans un courant défini. 4. Maupassant (1850 - 1893). Maître de la nouvelle, il fait son apprentissage auprès de Flaubert. 5. Hector Guimard (1867 - 1942). Architecte français qui imposa le style Art Nouveau, notamment grâce aux entrées du métropolitain. 6. William Morris (1834 - 1896). Décorateur, écrivain, peintre anglais. Le mouvement inspiré par Morris exerça une profonde influence sur l'Art Nouveau. 7. Le téléphone fut inventé par Alexander Bell en 1876. 8. Debussy (1862 - 1918). Compositeur français qui introduit une conception originale de l'harmonie et de la rythmique.

ANACHRONISMES IVème SIÈCLE AV.J.C.

Un jeu de culture générale au sens propre. Regarder une époque de façon générale et transversale afin de créer des liens entre les disciplines.Le but du jeu : repérer le personnage, fait ou objet qui ne fait pas partie de l'époque évoquée. C'est-à-dire chercher l'anachronisme

1.POLITIQUE Périclès
2.GUERRE Bataille de Marathon
3.GUERRE Guerre du Péloponnèse
4.LITTÉRATURE Plutarque
5.ARCHITECTURE Le Parthenon
6.PHILOSOPHIE Socrate
7.PHILOSOPHIE Platon
8.PHILOSOPHIE Aristote

HAND MADE

Le nom de «siècle de Périclès» a été donné à l'époque la plus brillante de la civilisation grecque.
1. Périclès (-495 à -429), stratège athénien, il monopolisa la scène politique pendant trente ans. 2. Bataille de Marathon (-490), première victoire grecque sur les Perses. Le messager, envoyé pour annoncer la victoire serait tombé mort d'épuisement en arrivant à Athènes. 3. Guerre du Péloponnèse (-431 à -404) opposa Athènes à Spartes et précipita le déclin de la cité. 4. Plutarque (46 à 125), biographe et moraliste grec. Anachronique par rapport au siècle de Périclès. 5. Le Parthenon (-447 à -432), temple d'Athéna et monument le plus prestigieux de l'Acropole fut édifié à l'instigation de Périclès. 6. Socrate (-470 à -399), philosophe grec. Condamné à mort pour avoir perverti la jeunesse avec «l'ironie socratique». 7. Platon (-428 à -348), élève de Socrate, il créa l'Académie où il enseigna la méthode dialectique et examina les insti-tutions politiques. 8. Aristote (-384 à -322), élève de Platon, précepteur d'Alexandre le Grand. Il fonda l'école du Lycée.

ANACHRONISMES LE RÈGNE DE LOUIS XIV

Un jeu de culture générale au sens propre. Regarder une époque de façon générale et transversale afin de créer des liens entre les disciplines.Le but du jeu : repérer le personnage, fait ou objet qui ne fait pas partie de l'époque évoquée. C'est-à-dire chercher l'anachronisme

1.POLITIQUE Colbert
2.GUERRE Traités de Westphalie
3.PHILOSOPHIE Cromwell
4.BEAUX-ARTS Velasquez
5.DÉCOUVERTE Montgolfière
6.LITTÉRATURE La Fontaine
7.ARCHITECTURE Le Nôtre
8.MUSIQUE Purcell

HAND MADE

Le règne du Roi Soleil : 1643 - 1715
1. Colbert (1619-1683). D'abord au service de Mazarin, puis de Louis XIV, il donna son nom au colbertisme : une application des principes mercantilistes. 2. Traités de Westphalie (1648). Pacte qui mit fin à la guerre de Trente Ans et consolida le morcellement de l'Allemagne. 3. Cromwell (1599-1658). Homme politique anglais qui lutta avec les puritains contre l'arbitraire monarchique. Il fit exécuter Charles I et instaura une République qui ne dura que onze ans. 4. Velasquez (1599-1660). Peintre espagnol. Parfois considéré comme un lointain précurseur de l'impressionisme. 5. Montgolfière (1783). Anachronisme. Les frères Montgolfier effectuèrent leur première ascension en 1783. 6. La Fontaine (1621-1695). Poète français, auteur des Fables, apologues inspirés d'Esope et écrit d'une plume rare. 7. Le Nôtre (1613-1700). Jardinier français, créateur du jardin dit "à la française". Il dessina notamment les jardins de Vaux-le-Vicomte et de Versailles. 8. Purcell (1658-1695). Seul grand compositeur que l'Angleterre a vu naître. Marqué par Lully, il exercera une influence certaine sur Haendel.

ANACHRONISMES LA GUERRE DE CENT ANS

Un jeu de culture générale au sens propre. Regarder une époque de façon générale et transversale afin de créer des liens entre les disciplines.Le but du jeu : repérer le personnage, fait ou objet qui ne fait pas partie de l'époque évoquée. C'est-à dire chercher l'anachronisme.

1.GUERRE Chute de Constantinople
2.GUERRE Tamerlan
3.POLITIQUE Jeanne d'Arc
4.BEAUX-ARTS Ming
5.INVENTION Gutenberg
6.SOCIÉTÉ La Peste Noire
7.RELIGION Le Grand Schisme
8.LITTÉRATURE Dante

HAND MADE

La guerre de Cent Ans opposa épisodiquement la France à l'Angleterre de 1328 à 1453.
1. Chute de Constantinople (1453). Les Ottomans mettent fin à l'Empire Romain Orientale. Constantinople devient Istanbul. 2. Tamerlan (1336 - 1405). Conquérant mongol sanguinaire. Il pille même Delhi en 1398. 3. Jeanne d'Arc (1412 - 1431). Brûlée vive par les Anglais. Fallait-il le rappeler? Pas plus que la victoire d'Azincourt en 1415. 4. La dynastie d'origine Ming supplanta celle des Yuan mongols en 1368. L'art chinois, notamment la céramique, renoua avec l'antique tradition. 5. Gutenberg (1400 - 1468). Imprimeur allemand, inventeur de la presse à imprimer (1434) avec des caractères métalliques. 6. La Peste Noire (1348 - 1350). Elle tue le quart ou le tiers de la population européenne en trois ans. 7. Le Grand Schisme (1328 - 1450) divise l'Eglise entre deux obédiences - «clémentine» en Avignon, «urbainiste» à Rome. 8. Dante (1265 - 1321). Pour les besoins du jeu, c'est un anachronisme. Mais de peu. La Divine Comédie fut écrite entre 1307 et sa mort.

Rarely Given Answers

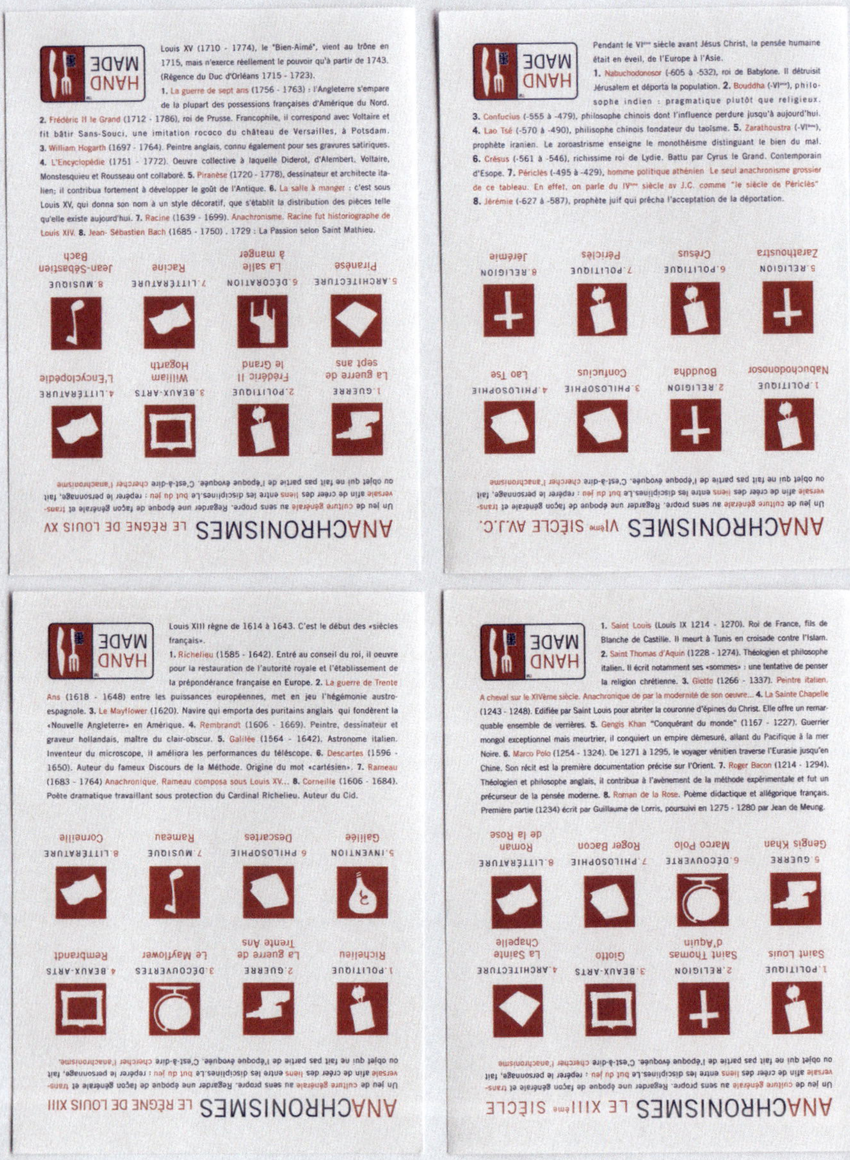
ANACHRONISMES LE RÈGNE DE LOUIS XV
Un jeu de culture générale au sens propre. Regarder une époque de façon générale et transversale afin de créer des liens entre les disciplines. Le but du jeu : repérer le personnage, fait ou objet qui ne fait pas partie de l'époque évoquée. C'est-à-dire chercher l'anachronisme
1.GUERRE La guerre de sept ans
2.POLITIQUE Frédéric II le Grand
3.BEAUX-ARTS William Hogarth
4.LITTÉRATURE L'Encyclopédie
5.ARCHITECTURE Piranèse
6.DÉCORATION La salle à manger
7.LITTÉRATURE Racine
8.MUSIQUE Jean-Sébastien Bach
HAND MADE
Louis XV (1710 - 1774), le "Bien-Aimé", vient au trône en 1715, mais n'exerce réellement le pouvoir qu'à partir de 1743. (Régence du Duc d'Orléans 1715 - 1723).
1. La guerre de sept ans (1756 - 1763) : l'Angleterre s'empare de la plupart des possessions françaises d'Amérique du Nord.
2. Frédéric II le Grand (1712 - 1786), roi de Prusse. Francophile, il correspond avec Voltaire et fit bâtir Sans-Souci, une imitation rococo du château de Versailles, à Potsdam.
3. William Hogarth (1697 - 1764). Peintre anglais, connu également pour ses gravures satiriques.
4. L'Encyclopédie (1751 - 1772). Oeuvre collective à laquelle Diderot, d'Alembert, Voltaire, Montesquieu et Rousseau ont collaboré. 5. Piranèse (1720 - 1778), dessinateur et architecte italien; il contribua fortement à développer le goût de l'Antique. 6. La salle à manger : c'est sous Louis XV, qui donna son nom à un style décoratif, que s'établit la distribution des pièces telle qu'elle existe aujourd'hui. 7. Racine (1639 - 1699). Anachronisme. Racine fut historiographe de Louis XIV. 8. Jean-Sébastien Bach (1685 - 1750) . 1729 : La Passion selon Saint Mathieu.
ANACHRONISMES VIème SIÈCLE AV.J.C.
Un jeu de culture générale au sens propre. Regarder une époque de façon générale et transversale afin de créer des liens entre les disciplines. Le but du jeu : repérer le personnage, fait ou objet qui ne fait pas partie de l'époque évoquée. C'est-à-dire chercher l'anachronisme
1.POLITIQUE Nabuchodonosor
2.RELIGION Bouddha
3.PHILOSOPHIE Confucius
4.PHILOSOPHIE Lao Tse
5.RELIGION Zarathoustra
6.POLITIQUE Crésus
7.POLITIQUE Périclès
8.RELIGION Jérémie
HAND MADE
Pendant le VIème siècle avant Jésus Christ, la pensée humaine était en éveil, de l'Europe à l'Asie.
1. Nabuchodonosor (-605 à -532), roi de Babylone. Il détruisit Jérusalem et déporta la population. 2. Bouddha (-VIème), philosophe indien : pragmatique plutôt que religieux.
3. Confucius (-555 à -479), philosophe chinois dont l'influence perdure jusqu'à aujourd'hui.
4. Lao Tsé (-570 à -490), philosophe chinois fondateur du taoïsme. 5. Zarathoustra (-VIème), prophète iranien. Le zoroastrisme enseigne le monothéisme distinguant le bien du mal.
6. Crésus (-561 à -546), richissime roi de Lydie. Battu par Cyrus le Grand. Contemporain d'Esope. 7. Périclès (-495 à -429), homme politique athénien. Le seul anachronisme grossier de ce tableau. En effet, on parle du IVème siècle av J.C. comme "le siècle de Périclès"
8. Jérémie (-627 à -587), prophète juif qui prêcha l'acceptation de la déportation.
ANACHRONISMES LE RÈGNE DE LOUIS XIII
Un jeu de culture générale au sens propre. Regarder une époque de façon générale et transversale afin de créer des liens entre les disciplines. Le but du jeu : repérer le personnage, fait ou objet qui ne fait pas partie de l'époque évoquée. C'est-à-dire chercher l'anachronisme.
1.POLITIQUE Richelieu
2.GUERRE La guerre de Trente Ans
3.DÉCOUVERTES Le Mayflower
4.BEAUX-ARTS Rembrandt
5.INVENTION Galilée
6.PHILOSOPHIE Descartes
7.MUSIQUE Rameau
8.LITTÉRATURE Corneille
HAND MADE
Louis XIII règne de 1614 à 1643. C'est le début des «siècles français».
1. Richelieu (1585 - 1642). Entré au conseil du roi, il oeuvre pour la restauration de l'autorité royale et l'établissement de la prépondérance française en Europe. 2. La guerre de Trente Ans (1618 - 1648) entre les puissances européennes, met en jeu l'hégémonie austro-espagnole. 3. Le Mayflower (1620). Navire qui emporta des puritains anglais qui fondèrent la «Nouvelle Angleterre» en Amérique. 4. Rembrandt (1606 - 1669). Peintre, dessinateur et graveur hollandais, maître du clair-obscur. 5. Galilée (1564 - 1642). Astronome italien. Inventeur du microscope, il améliora les performances du télescope. 6. Descartes (1596 - 1650). Auteur du fameux Discours de la Méthode. Origine du mot «cartésien». 7. Rameau (1683 - 1764) Anachronique. Rameau composa sous Louis XV... 8. Corneille (1606 - 1684). Poète dramatique travaillant sous protection du Cardinal Richelieu. Auteur du Cid.
ANACHRONISMES LE XIIIème SIÈCLE
Un jeu de culture générale au sens propre. Regarder une époque de façon générale et transversale afin de créer des liens entre les disciplines. Le but du jeu : repérer le personnage, fait ou objet qui ne fait pas partie de l'époque évoquée. C'est-à-dire chercher l'anachronisme
1.POLITIQUE Saint Louis
2.RELIGION Saint Thomas d'Aquin
3.BEAUX-ARTS Giotto
4.ARCHITECTURE La Sainte Chapelle
5.GUERRE Gengis Khan
6.DÉCOUVERTE Marco Polo
7.PHILOSOPHIE Roger Bacon
8.LITTÉRATURE Roman de la Rose
HAND MADE
1. Saint Louis (Louis IX 1214 - 1270). Roi de France, fils de Blanche de Castille. Il meurt à Tunis en croisade contre l'Islam.
2. Saint Thomas d'Aquin (1228 - 1274). Théologien et philosophe italien. Il écrit notamment ses «sommes» : une tentative de penser la religion chrétienne. 3. Giotto (1266 - 1337). Peintre italien. A cheval sur le XIVème siècle. Anachronique de par la modernité de son oeuvre... 4. La Sainte Chapelle (1243 - 1248). Edifiée par Saint Louis pour abriter la couronne d'épines du Christ. Elle offre un remarquable ensemble de verrières. 5. Gengis Khan "Conquérant du monde" (1167 - 1227). Guerrier mongol exceptionnel mais meurtrier, il conquiert un empire démesuré, allant du Pacifique à la mer Noire. 6. Marco Polo (1254 - 1324). De 1271 à 1295, le voyager vénitien traverse l'Eurasie jusqu'en Chine. Son récit est la première documentation précise sur l'Orient. 7. Roger Bacon (1214 - 1294). Théologien et philosophe anglais, il contribua à l'avènement de la méthode expérimentale et fut un précurseur de la pensée moderne. 8. Roman de la Rose. Poème didactique et allégorique français. Première partie (1234) écrit par Guillaume de Lorris, poursuivi en 1275 - 1280 par Jean de Meung.

10 BRAND MEMORABILIA

Judging by the exhibitions that major luxury brands organise worldwide, you might think that part of branding is maintaining well organised archives. The saying *"if you want to know where you're going, look where you came from"* is very true. However, in general, I am dismayed at how little attention companies pay to the memory of their brand. The aforementioned luxury brands are currently investing heavily to buy back former goods and are busy creating archive museums to stock their history in ideal conditions.

Keeping daily and intelligently-pruned archives is almost a definition of brand content creation. All the drawings and photos in this book concerning HANDMADE™ obviously come from carefully organised archives.

T.S. Eliot's famous line from Four Quartets : « *time past and time future are both contained in time present* » applies perfectly to branding. <u>Brands must honour their past</u>, <u>embody the Zeitgest of the moment</u> <u>and endeavour to shape the future.</u> Easier said than done.

> In all things, go from the known to the unknown.
> Jean Guitton

Are beauty and memory separate things? Are things not beautiful because they are slightly familiar and resemble our memories?

Orhan Pamuk. Nobel Prize in literature 2006.

> *We do not keep in our memory homogeneous books, but fragments torn from partial readings, often mingled one with the other, and they are, moreover, reworked by our personal fantasies: snippets of falsified books.*
>
> Pierre Bayard.
> University professor and author.

Paying attention means making the present exist by wanting to use it in the future, because we only memorize what we intend to reuse. Contrary to what we think, memory is not knowledge in the past tense. It's about the project, the future. Alain Sotto. Psychologist in education.

The real goal of memory is to optimize decision-making. It's important that the brain forgets irrelevant details and instead focuses on the stuff that's going to help make decisions in the real world.
Blake Richards. Toronto University.

A memory is the most important thing for a brand.
Claudio Luti. Managing Director of Kartell.

For Henri Bergson, forgetting is indispensable for action. The brain only lets through memories that are useful for immediate action.
Antoine Lejeune. Neurologist.

A source of inspiration for designers and heritage for brands, fashion archives have become a major issue for the big names in luxury.
Emmanuelle Bosc. Journalist.

We only see what we've already seen.
Jean Guitton

Memories should be turned into projects.
Pierre Bergé

To highlight a brand's uniqueness in a plethoric offer, talking about DNA has become a catchphrase. The necessity to build an authentic memory is now essential.
Emmanuelle Bosc. Journalist.

Knowing is remembering.
Aristotle

P.S. The future is built on the past

11 EMOTIONS RULE

A few years ago, when cosmetic companies based their advertising principally on scientific tests, I presented to the Executive Committee an advert that had been made by a cameraman specialised in shooting slow-motion chocolate films. The Commercial Director immediately retorted: " but emotion doesn't sell!".
I didn't have the research that is available today to prove my point scientifically, but we pushed on and the campaign was a roaring success.

Sometimes it is perhaps better not to say anything at all. Roald Dahl gives this advice to whomsoever has the privilege to drink a glass of Romanée-Conti : " Smell that perfume! Breathe in that bouquet! Taste it! Drink it. But never try to describe it! It's impossible to put such a delight into words! "

Evoke and provoke, rather than show and demonstrate.

Hugh Wilson

WE ALL GREW UP LEARNING THAT MAN HAS A BRAIN.
And yet, according to our current medical knowledge,
we have three: one in the head, one in the intestines and
one in the heart. While the brain in the head is the largest,
the brain in the intestine has as many neurones as a cat
and the brain in the heart as many as a laboratory rat.

Frédéric Therin. *Influencia*.

*All true emotion is a lie in the intellect,
for it is not in the intellect that it takes place.*
Pessoa

Thanks to social broadcasting networks, everyone
and everything is its own brand. Now we want
the one thing the Internet can't buy : human emotion.
Facts are out, feelings are in.

Branding is supposedly not about what something says,
or what it means, but how it makes us feel.

When we talk about a strong brand, what we mean
is that it consistently delivers the emotion it promises.
The most successful brands successfully use design
to produce an emotional coherence that spans content
to product to experience. Not everything has to look alike,
but it all has to feel alike. Whenever we encounter them
we get that familiar brand sensation. That tingling tells
you it's working.

When everything is available all the time and we're
inundated with information in every way, shape and form,
we're left no choice but to favour what makes us feel.

Michael Rock

Rembrandt said just six words about his art – that he wanted to create " the greatest and most natural movement ". He meant, surely, emotion as well as motion. Jackie Wullschläger

> Emotion is to decision what posture
> is to gesture: a tool to prepare for action.
> Alain Berthoz. Neurophysiologist.

I'm like Paris-Match. Immediate emotion, that's what I'm looking for. When Picasso painted Guernica, did he go round in circles? Gérard Rancinan. Photographer.

> I'm not interested in colour. It evokes a specific emotion. I'm not trying to deal with emotion, I'm trying to deal with awe. I'm interested in that bigger space. Mohammed Qasim Ashfaq

Intuition and instinct are the only things we know for sure. Hiro. Photographer.

No Lexus engineer is unaware of the «waku doki» concept, theorised by Toyota's president. While the teams still maintain high technological quality, they must now ensure that their cars also provoke «a rush of adrenaline and heartbeats» for their customers.

Yann Rousseau

Godard says that «you hear before you see». For my part, I often have the impression that I recognize at the same time as I discover.

Sarah Moon

*Feel shapes,
smell noises,*

form follows feelings.
— Jacob Jensen

Non cogito, ergo sum. *Intelligent Life*

What's visceral is irrefutable. Apollinaire

Colour links us with cosmic regions. Paul Klee

*see flavours,
hear colours.* — Alan Fletcher

The eye listens.*

It's what I do that shows me what I'm looking for. Pierre Soulages

An emotion, or rather that motion of the spirit. Jean Guitton

*Paul Claudel

Proven: Emotions trump thoughts

SENSATIONS → EMOTIONS
HANDMADE

Most emotions are of little use in branding: anger, disgust, fear and sadness don't trigger many sales. The simple – and very personal - theory I used for HANDMADE™ is that you can create happiness (*the only positive emotion category*) by touching more than one sense at a time. Just as brands that collaborate use a multiplication sign to express the added value of their joint partnership, I tried to touch as many senses as possible in order to create positive feelings all along the shopper's journey around the restaurant : sight, smell, hearing, taste and touch. The so-called sixth sense probably understands unseen details and intentions and may well be the most important of all. As everybody has their own favourite sense and good-feeling-combination, it is probably advisable to maximise the number of sensations to try and create a positive emotion in as many people as possible.

Opposite I have listed the senses a visitor to HANDMADE™ *might have been sensitive to.*

HEARING
HANDMADE™ only ever played British music
(Pink Floyd, The Rolling Stones, Massive Attack etc.)

TOUCH
The fridge, counter and shelves were made
of grey Italian Pietra Serena stone, the floor
of beige Burgandy Buxy stone. The tables, benches
and trays were made of solid oak. The glasses
were handblown in Normandy, the pottery
handmade in Burgundy. The sign was painted
by a signwriter. The white paint was matt.

SMELL
Illy coffee, homemade soup and apple crumble
were probably the most common fragrances
in the air.

TASTE
Homemade chutneys and marmalades.
Montgomery cheddar, Colston Basset stilton,
home-smoked beef and salmon. Even the
simplest of meals had the finest ingredients.

SIGHT
All the objects mentioned under "touch" were
as beautiful to look at as they were pleasant
to feel. The grey, beige and white colours created
backdrops to highlight the products themselves.
The still life photography and visual identity were
conceived to thrill.

SIXTH SENSE
Humour, lightheartedness and attention
to detail were, I hope, the HANDMADE™
attitude to business.

12 THE *FINE LINE* EFFECT

Today knowledge travels so fast and freely that cars, smartphones and perfumes end up looking very much like those of their competitors. Sometimes the only apparent distinction between fashion brand adverts seems to be the logo; the models and photographers being often interchangeable, if not identical.

That being said, small differences can and do make a big difference. I call it *The Fine Line Effect*.

Virgil Abloh, Louis Vuitton's former Art Director and founder of Off White, even put a percentage on the Fine Line Effect, when he declared that a 3% change is sufficient to create a new object.

> Perhaps part of the pleasure in the game of distinction is playing "spot the difference" and the smaller the nuance between two things, the greater the amusement. It is indeed probably more interesting to compare two vintages of the same Chablis Grand Cru, rather than compare a Meursault to a Montrachet.

DIFFERENCE

Even a solitary accent can transmogrify a word from one language to another.

DIFFÉRENCE

> " TO BE **DIFFERENT** OR NOT TO BE, THAT IS THE ~~QUESTION~~ **ANSWER**. "

There are several ways of creating The Fine Line Effect.
A slight change in scale, perspective, context or texture can
radically transform the initial idea and create something novel.

There's only a very fine line between two
completely different nations.

There's only a very fine line between two
completely different notions.

A perfumer I know who once worked on reproducing
the aroma of Romanée Conti told me that the smell of a cheap
and nasty tablewine was only 0,001% difference away
from that of Burgundy's most famous wine.

One **hair makes a difference.**
Claude Brouet

The layout of the subject *is new*.
Blaise Pascal

The difference is often *not great*, but it is *crucial*.
Roy Lichtenstein

***Newness* is what was forgotten.**
Rose Bertin

He who does not imitate, *does not invent*.
Alain

Fashion is *a question of centimetres*.
Jean-Paul Gaultier

CONNAÎTRE, C'EST RECONNAÎTRE.

[understanding is recognising]

The play on words, the alliteration and the mnemomics in this French quotation by Jean Guitton are unfortunately totally lost in English.

You only have to look at one of Michelangelo's heads to understand that the most astonishing inventions are extremely close to the thing itself, so close to the ordinary in fact, that it is only the craftsman without genius who reveals the difference. This is also true of the great poets, who say things that are quite common, in everyday words, and in the most natural way. The inimitable resembles the commonplace.

Alain. Philosopher.

HANDMADE

Apparently there's a fine line between what I considered an attractive and amusing window poster and what the Parisian Financial Times correspondent considered a breach of copyright!

Instead of doing the obvious and photographing a salad in a bowl, the idea here was to change context and show only the salad seeds. There is also a somewhat gender-offensive joke in the name. The French actually do have a salad named: « fat lazy blonde ».

Texture is the single most important aspect of quality.
John Pawson

I brought Irving Penn's " Italian Ingredients " photograph as inspiration for the HANDMADE™ " Cheddar Sandwich " shoot with Guido Mocafico. (cf p 178/179) " You can't just copy Penn! ", Guido exclaimed, and proceeded to simply change the camera's perspective, from vertical to horizontal, thereby creating a totally novel photograph. 90° is a very large angle difference, you may say.

In short : Small changes make a big difference

EN
PR
D

13

13 ENTREPRENDRE

Entrepreneur is a French word. The verb, *"entreprendre"* literally speaking means *"enter and take!"*, which is precisely what entrepreneurs must do.

You only get what you take.
You only eat what you kill.

It might sound arrogant or pedantic to want to change the world, improve people's lives and bring joy to your customers. But those are precisely the aspirations that entrepreneurs bring to the market. What you choose to do needs to be what matters to you most. It also requires sufficiently high margins to enable you to work on developing the business. Insufficient profits will force you to work in the business, not on it, thereby jeopardising your brand's future.

IT'S ALWAYS DAY ONE

Day 2 is stasis.
Followed by irrelevance.
Followed by excruciating, painful decline.
Followed by death.
And that is why it is always Day 1.

Jeff Bezos

I predict that one day Amazon will die. If you look at the big companies, their life expectancy tends to be thirty years or more, not a hundred years or more.

Jeff Bezos

THE ENTREPRENEUR

Inside the owner of every small business there is a three-way battle going on between the entrepreneur, the manager, and the technician. The entrepreneur is the visionary in us. The manager is pragmatic. The technician is the doer. We all have a little of each inside us. If they were equally balanced, we would be describing an incredibly confident individual.
Michael E Gerber

> Tim Harford says that entrepreneurs need "*sunny overconfidence*" in order to persevere undaunted by the high chances of failure.

The entrepreneur's survival kit includes

and independence,
enthusiasm,
optimism,
tenacity,
flair,
the ability to rebuild immediately after a failure. **Eléna Fourès**

If there are no competitors, then the market is not yet here.
Tanguy de La Fouchardière

The first thing to do when creating a start-up is to determine its purpose. If you don't know in what way the world will be a better place because of your company, your chances of building a very successful one are small.
Bill Aulet. MIT.

The large companies of tomorrow are those whose ambition exceeds their activity. **Alexandre Bompard**

The interior of the HANDMADE™ restaurant, April 1999. Burgandy Buxy stone floor; solid light oak tables & benches; grey Pietra Serena marble for the counter and fridge.

THE DEADLY SINS OF HANDMADE™

Pioneers are rarely winners that take all.
To get a simple message into people's heads
often requires a lot of repetition.

Timing is everything.
[*the right product in the right place* at the right time*]
Nobody cares. As Banksy says : " No one is completely
unhappy when their best friends fail " .

**Readiness to observe, listen and learn; then pivot
and change, is key to success.**
People are naturally critically suspicious : " Oh! Your brand is
called handmade. That must mean it's industrial. " [sic]

**Consumers are interested in themselves
and their thoughts; not in you and yours.**
There are invisible commercial rules in every street,
shop by shop. Certain addresses seem to have little
or no potential and be permanently jinxed.

**Consumers chiefly buy an end product,
not your idiosyncratic view on life.**
Good locations can become bad ones overnight, for any
number of reasons, all of them completely out of your control.

**Nobody cares if your delivery van breaks down,
all they want is food on time.**
You're the boss, but that makes you both responsible
and accountable for everything that goes wrong.

**Cultural Added Value needs to be funded by high
margins. [cf Bernard Arnault & François Pinault]**

*The old saying : location, location, location, still holds true.

ENTREPRENDRE

You pay for every mistake. In cash.

Entrepreneurs should not forget the basic needs of their spouses, partners and children.

It takes generations, literally, to change people's habits. Old habits die very hard indeed.

Consumers unmercifully compare your goods and services to all those already in your market.

People's preconceived ideas are almost impossible to change.

Great press reviews have very little connection to the reality of the Profit & Loss account.

You need a plan A, a plan B and most importantly, a plan C. C as in catastrophe.

Trust your first gut reaction when hiring people.

A young entrepreneur friend of mine says: if plan A fails, make a new plan A!

Having associates often leads to problems; but being all by yourself can be tricky too.

Gesamtkunstwerk* teaches us that you'd better start a business you would enjoy working in, without being paid, for long hours. Because that is what will happen. At best for quite some time. At worst, for ever.

10% of 100 is twice that of 100% of 5.

You get paid late. And last.

Whatever sector of activity you choose, you automatically become an accountant, a lawyer, head of human relations and the person who cleans the Water Closet.

*cf chapter 41 GESAMTKUNSTWERK

Believe me! Startuppers become Davids versus Goliaths

14 FAVOURABLE CONDITIONS

I once complained to a friend that someone I deemed incompetent had just been promoted to CEO. "Yes, but that person did everything they possibly could to get the job", he replied.

This sounds obvious, but it is so true and it is as true for people as it is for brands. To be productive in an open space, sit next to someone who is hardworking, *just as you should open your shop next door to your competitor.*

David Hockney owes his revolutionary and historical discovery of the role of optical devices in painting to his workshop's 70 metre-long wall, upon which he had pinned photocopies of the entire history of painting. "*My Great Wall allowed me to see, with one sweep of the eye, that the optical look arrived suddenly and was immediately coherent and complete*" he writes in *Secret Knowledge*.

In order to create the perfect conditions prior to writing, Gustave Flaubert would spend a whole day cutting up to 200 goose quills in preparation. Nadar, the pioneer French photographer of the XIXth century built a large glasshouse on top of a building in Paris in order to obtain maximum daylight for his art. Even Francis Bacon's litter-strewn workshop was conducive to his manner of painting. Claude Monet could never have produced his "Nymphéas" paintings from a garret. Go and visit his studio in Giverney, it's enormous. Richard Thaler, the Nobel Prize Winner for his work on behavioural economics, underlines scientifically just how strongly conditions influence results. A fly painted on an urinal nudges men to aim at the insect rather than wet the floor. And in a charming TED talk, Ken Robinson gave a striking example of favourable conditions where he reminds us that, given the right meteorological conditions, flowers can blossom even in Death Valley.

Give your brand optimum chances for success by creating the most favourable conditions possible.

It's surprising how much one can achieve with
a few elementary writing tools; and a computer.

CONDITIONS FOR *TRUST*

One of the most memorable seminars I ever attended was in Hamburg, Germany. "Dialog im Dunkeln" [Dialogue in the Dark] invite people to discover the world of complete darkness. Over the two-day event our management team spent several sessions in pitch black, guided and coached by blind people. The message I learned, very forcibly, was that for blind people "trust is the only option". As soon as you step into a lightless room, you too become totally dependent on your fellow colleagues. Each person is linked by hand to the person in front and behind, like alpine climbers roped together, and as you overcome obstacles, you give friendly advice to those following.
But even the blind do not give blind trust.

Sir Alex Ferguson believes that if you give people total loyalty and trust, they will give it back to you. However, whenever his trust was broken, he would briskly fire any player who aspired to take over control in Manchester United's dressing room.

The French are statistically, so the studies say, a highly suspicious and distrustful nation. I have however, in over forty years in France and with only two notable exceptions in mind, found that if you give trust, you get it back.

> Through complete trust, we can make it impossible for somebody to deceive us.
> Joseph Joubert

God gave men both a penis and a brain, but unfortunately not enough blood supply to run both at the same time.

Robbie Williams

What makes Apple special is not so much that it designed the iPod or iPhone as that it created the conditions for these products to come into being. How did they do that? By putting design at the heart of production. Jean-Guillaume Santi

Be regular and orderly in your life like a bourgeois, so that you can be violent and original in your work.

Gustave Flaubert

On my scholar's dream stone, which I brought back from China, I contemplate the natural design of the mineral; I see landscapes, limpid springs, mountains in formation, morning mists... In search of inspiration, they help to nourish my thoughts, to restructure my inner space and to animate my imagination.

Fabienne Verdier.

It was his own fault, or instead, his mistake. He should not have built the fire under the pine tree. He should have built it in an open space. The snow fell without warning upon the man and the fire, and the fire was dead.

Jack London.

Ready? Prepare and anticipate

15 REALITY RULES

The author, aged 16 on the river *La Durance* in France.

A few moments later, reality really did rule. I inadvertently got caught sideways against a rock and the weight of the rushing water crushed the fibreglass to smithereens. I lived to tell the tale...

15 REALITY RULES

Every game starts with an explanation of the rules.
You are not allowed to touch the ball with your hands
in football; you can't pass the ball forwards in rugby.
One is however inclined to forget the elementary rules
of commerce in the excitement of creating a brand.
The playing field in any sector is anything but level.
That is an unfortunate, but given, fact of life.

To take the finger food business as a case in point, customers know the unwritten rules and regulations of any street better than you do. They can even enforce what you might at first consider "unfair" practices upon you. For example, people in Paris readily accept the fact that McDonald's don't give change back on Restaurant Vouchers. However, if one bakery in your street accepts to give change back, then those same clients who willingly accept McDonald's national policies will threaten to boycott your eating house. Customers are merciless in their decision taking. We all are, actually. People compare the value for money, speed and professionalism of your brand's offering to those in the nearby neighbourhood. I opened up my finger food restaurant near two bakers selling sandwiches made with their own bread and an up-market Delicatessen chain with a centralised kitchen.

Needless to say, margins are higher if you're not buying in bread from outside and if you can spread your kitchen's overheads across several outlets.
The simple conclusion is that the dice are heavily loaded before a start-up even opens its doors for business.
"Barriers to entry" is the technical expression.

One beautiful summer's day I was riding my motorbike on the motorway when I sensed a burning smell come through my helmet. I immediately thought it must be a farmer burning a field of stubble. A second or two later, an enormous burning rubber wheel flew off a lorry I was overtaking, straight at me. The tyre just grazed my exhaust pipe as it sped past, leaving a line of burnt rubber as a souvenir. There was nothing I could have done. It was just pure luck that I escaped. Then again, I thought later, had I realised that the smell was burning rubber and not corn stubble, I would have paid more attention to the vehicles around me. I suppose the moral I take from this experience is that you need to be on your guard all the time.

On a motorbike or in a brand, keep your eyes peeled for what may well be coming round the corner.

As fate or irony would have it, I am writing these particular lines during the Coronavirus lockdown. Having spent a year and a half preparing this project with Axel Vagnard, my Art Director, we were perfectly poised to work from afar. Perhaps I've learnt to be on my guard after all.

To ZIG or to ZAG,
that is the question...

...to ZIGZAG
has to be the answer.

CHANGING (BREAKING) RULES

"Jump and a net will appear" is an expression I read before opening HANDMADE™ and that I no doubt took somewhat too much at face value.
Today, I would propose: *"jump and you will probably fall"*, or more optimistically, *" look before you leap"*.

For brands, reality tends to be more cruel than it is kind. The law of the strongest, richest or biggest often holds true. Disruption often admittedly comes from the small, but the conclusion is the same: YOU HAVE TO BE READY FOR ANYTHING THAT IS THROWN AT YOU.

There was an unbelievable motorbike Grand Prix in 2015 at Assen in Holland, between Valentino Rossi and Marc Marquez. Both pilots were wheel to wheel in the last couple of corners having already overtaken each other dozens of times during the race. On the final chicane, Marquez infamously gave Rossi a nudge, sending the Italian onto the soft sandy protective surface, where pilots can break their fall if they miss a corner. As everybody knows, or can guess, coming off the hard asphalt onto an unstable gravelly ground is the perfect recipe for a tumble.
Rossi somehow and famously, in a millionth of a second, had the presence of mind to hold his handlebars steady and almost fly, in a straight line, over the stones and back onto the track, just in front of his opponent, to win the race. It is the perfect example of changing the rules of the game, without even breaking them.

> The motorbike doesn't fall. *You do. Ride with it.*
> **Hugh Wilson**

Everybody has a plan until they get punched in the mouth.

Mike Tyson

Talking of breaking the rules, without wanting to encourage entrepreneurs to become outlaws, or tread on too many people's toes, it has to be said that it is difficult for a start-up to abide rigorously by the law.

The recent expression " *hacking growth* " encourages what Steve Jobs would probably call a pirate mindset. *Common decency and common sense are again called upon to steer a middle course.*

It takes all the running you can do, to keep in the same place. If you want to get somewhere else, you must run at least twice as fast as that !

The Queen-of-Hearts. Lewis Carroll.

XXXXX is very much a fashion business. And so when things are in fashion, fine, and when they go out of fashion, not so fine.

Bernard Arnault.
Chairman of LVMH.

Motorcycling requires you to manoeuvre through the density of reality.

Matthew B Crawford. Philosopher.

I don't want to change the rules of the game, I want to change the game.

André Breton.
Co-founder of Surrealism.

Reality : Uncertainty and unfairness are the norm

16

ORDNUNG
IST DAS HALBE LEBEN
ORDER IS HALF OF LIFE

" Ordnung ist das halbe Leben! " a German intern once proclaimed, as if it were a proverb to be observed scrupulously.
I checked recently on internet and found that for Germans it probably is. Apparently *" Ordnung muss sein "* [There must be order] is a variant of the above. At the time I should have replied : *" Perhaps, but here in France, mess is definitely the other half of life "* .

But we were working in a fragrance company, where almost every employee, except the perfumers themselves, probably did spend half of their time organising perfumes into families. And each fragrance house has its own specific perfume mapping system. How the Brand Managers in the luxury perfume sector deal with being sold different classifications of the same fragrance is quite another story.

The cult of tidiness, spearheaded by Marie Kendo – the Japanese guru of order – probably says more about our consumer society's clutter than the necessity for brands to devote half of their time to matters of order. Half of life is a German exaggeration, I hope, but the success of brands such as Zara, Amazon and Google definitely depends on manic logistical order.

Filing is already thinking.
Advert for Exacompta, stationery manufacturers.

On an individual level, the way people organise their thoughts sketches their self-portrait. I was told by a friend in China that certain Chinese classify their ideas around proverbs. The French author Georges Perec wrote a book entitled "Think/Classify" that encourages people to create their own classification methods. I can fully understand both of these attitudes as this book itself clusters thoughts around topics that I consider vital for better branding.

To have and to hold stimulating thoughts is part of a Brand's equity. This necessarily requires a certain amount of organisational discipline and choice of system. But as ever, mess (chaos ?) - the other side of the Ordnung coin – also has its role to play in stimulating brand creativity. Another German concept, that perfectly counterbalances the first and could be printed on side B of our proverbial Deutschmark, is "kreatives Chaos".

As often the answer lies in flipping the coin from heads to tails on a regular basis.

The joy of classification.
Roland Barthes. Semiotician.

Mix : Balance order and disorder

FOR ORDER

THE PSYCHOLOGY OF GENRE

The human brain is a pattern-matching machine. When we put things into a category, research has found, they actually become more alike in our minds. Things we might have viewed as more similar become, when placed into two distinct categories, more different. We don't like what we find hard to categorize. And the more we like something, the more we like to categorize it.

Tom Vanderbilt. Journalist and author.

Where there is order there is a well-being.

LE CORBUSIER. ARCHITECT.

From the very first step, that of classification (you have to classify and sample, if you want to build up a corpus) photography remains elusive.

Roland Barthes. Semiotician.

With everything being digital these days we're going to be a generation of lost records.

Olympia Scarry. Artist.

If you don't remove the sand from your life every day…

Henri Thomas.
French author and poet.

*There all is order and beauty,
luxury, peace and pleasure.*

Charles Baudelaire

For every minute spent in organising an hour is earned.

Benjamin Franklin

The curiosity cabinet disappeared because
it mixed things that were meant to be separated
or classified. Contrary to popular belief,
the curiosity cabinet is not chaos: on the contrary,
it is an attempt to comprehend the world.
We all have a curiosity cabinet within us.

Laurent Le Bon. Art historian.

FOR MESS

The primary interest of mess is to provide *intellectual stimulation.* **The messy person has a strong relationship to objects. His** *powers of evocation are unparalleled,* **and his** *fantasy world is much more intense as well.*

Laurence Einfalt. Psychologist.

If a cluttered desk is a sign of a cluttered mind, of what then, is an empty desk a sign? Albert Einstein

Out of sight, out of mind.
[Atelier rangé, esprit dérangé]
Didier Barbotte. Mechanic in Burgundy.

One of the advantages of being disorderly is that one is constantly making exciting discoveries.

A.A. Milne

Disorder is the true motor of man, at the same time as progress.

Nassim Nicolas Taleb. Mathematical statistician and author.

I couldn't live without my bohemian surroundings - books, magazines, newspapers ... and mess.

Yves Saint Laurent

I like things to permeate my being, without rhyme or reason, and organise themselves.

Jean-Luc Mélanchon. French politician.

Finding a man's home with no mess is like looking into his eyes and finding no soul.

Hugo MacDonald. Consultant and journalist.

Put them away, sort them out? How horrible! I prefer to spread them out.

Grégoire Solotareff. Image Maker.

The messy employee is more productive because he takes 36% less time than his Cartesian colleague to get his hands on a document among the piles littering his desk.

Eric Abrahamson. Professor at Columbia Business School, New York.

BALANCED MESS AND ORDER

Disorder is very, very close to order.
It's a bus ticket away from total chaos.
And that's what I like, really.

Michael Palin. Monty Python founding member.

**Be regular and orderly
in your life like a bourgeois,
so that you can be violent
and original in your work.**

Gustave Flaubert

Le Corbusier's atelier is full
of creative chaos, but the living areas
are ordered and comfortable.

Harriet Agnew. Journalist.

**Too much organisation
is a trap.
Say thank you to old ideas
before discarding them.
Consider each idea, and ask
"Does it spark joy?"
Only then should you keep it.**

Hugh Wilson after Marie Kondo

The present order is the disorder of the future.

Ian Hamilton Finlay. Artist.

17 ALL WORK AND YES PLAY

WHICHEVER SECTOR OF ACTIVITY YOU CONSIDER, THERE IS NO ALTERNATIVE TO HARD WORK.

Churchill's offer of toil and sweat, hopefully without the blood, but maybe with a few tears, sums up hard work. Sir Winston himself wrote more words in his lifetime than Dickens and Shakespeare combined. David Bowie "could not but work". And Karl Lagerfeld described himself, not as a workaholic or a Stakhanovist, but as a work nymphomaniac, perpetually dissatisfied.

The secret of success is undoubtedly grit, grind and grafting. Anders Ericsson even puts a number on it, claiming that it takes 10.000 hours to become an expert. Ferdinand Cheval spent 33 years building his "Ideal Palace". But then passionate people don't count their hours. When what you do becomes a passion and an obsession, then the perseverant long hours of labour become your natural pastime. And what you do naturally, easily and often, is probably what people most value from you, too.

In order for Jack not to become a dull boy - or Nicholson a mad man - pauses, breaks and rests are essential. It's a question of managing recuperation. From Descartes' theory of dividing problems into their smallest common denominators, to Lao Tzu's thousand-mile journey, the value of breaking work down into small, bite-sized tasks or steps is universally acknowledged.
As Kevin Ashton says: "most steps wins".

Real-work time is short. He who can only pay attention for ten minutes at a time can still do a lot, if he renews his effort, like rowers who rest for a moment after each stroke of the oar.

Jean Guitton. Philosopher and theologian.

I'm a digger. I do things over and over again, even now. I sit at my drawing board and I think until it comes. Either it comes or it doesn't. I draw musicians, in the meantime, to please myself. It takes days, sometimes even months, to come up with an idea. Awful! Anyone who worked as hard as I do could do better.

Sempé. Cartoonist.

One must work, if not out of taste, at least out of desperation, since, all things considered, working is less boring than having fun.

Baudelaire

Michael Phelps [record number of Olympic gold medals] admitted to a journalist that his only concern was re-cu-pe-ra-tion.

I don't like work - nobody likes it - **but I like what work contains -** *the chance to find yourself.* Joseph Conrad

There is something fractal about rest: we need it daily, weekly and yearly.

Tim Harford. Economist and journalist.

Upon awakening, you should instantly seize your mind and force it, without giving it time for distraction, to knuckle down to work right away, even whilst washing, and drag your body to the work table, sit it down pen in hand without giving it the chance to resist.

Jules Payot. French educationist. 1859-1940.

Counsel. Work hard playfully

Minds do not leap.
Observation, evaluation,
and iteration,
not sudden shifts of perception,
solve problems
and lead us to creation.
We move from know
to new in small steps.
Find a problem, solve it,
and repeat.
Most steps wins.

↑
Kevin Ashton.
Technology pioneer. →

Work itself is a treasure. Jean de La Fontaine
Work is much more fun than fun. Noël Coward
It's just work, like planing a plank. Jacques Brel
It's only pain. Jürgen Klopp. Liverpool Coach.
He who has begun has half done. Horace
Begin again and you're done. Jean Guitton
I've erased my work behind me, but it exists.
Louis-Ferdinand Céline

The best way to begin is the same as the best way to swim in the sea. No tiptoes. No wading. Go under. Get wet and cold from scalp to sole. Do not look back or think ahead. Just go. In the beginning, all that matters is how much clay you throw on the wheel. Go for as many hours as you can. Repeat every day possible until you die. A thing begun is less right than wrong, more flaw than finesse, all problem and no solution. Nothing begins good, but everything good begins. Everything can be revised, erased, or rearranged later. The courage of creation is making bad beginnings.

18 EVOLVING EVERYDAY

" Little strokes fell great oaks" goes the saying. Building a brand, as with any skill or job, takes time, patience and continual, relentless perseverance.

This is hardly a new idea, but it is sometimes comforting to know that every creator is obliged to submit to the law of building brick by brick, little by little. And the cook's rule of *"clean as you go"* is as simple and true as it is applicable in all walks of life and all sectors of activity.

Sufficient unto the day is the evil thereof. Matthew chapter 6, verse 34.

Like Daedalus, I am making wings. I compose them little by little, and add a feather every day. Joseph Joubert

Weaving the web of days.
Algernon Charles Swinburne

The pursuit of mastery is an ever-onward almost.
Sarah Lewis

The secret of brand success is constant restlessness. John Hegarty

To maintain a brand you have to renew it perpetually. Claude Terrail

The measure of man is the way he seizes the day.

Ralph Waldo Emerson

Kaizen is the Japanese word for "continual improvement."

Little is enough each day if each day acquires that little..
Bossuet

Nulla dies sine linea
[Never a day without a line].

Leonardo, the maestro of endless change.
Holland Cotter

Daily: Be regular, open and persistent

MANAGEMENT RULES OF THUMB

When gardeners, armed with chainsaws, prune chestnut trees in Paris, they follow a string line. A length of twine attached between two poles. When they leave, the trees in the avenue look as if they have been cut with a laser beam. String lines, like rules of thumb are short-sharp-simple* rules that are easy to understand and provide robust guidelines. For centuries, masons and carpenters have built beautiful vernacular houses using only their hands, feet and thumbs as measuring sticks.

Management is about creating the conditions that make life and work easy for all.

Overcomplicated rules & regulations produce the opposite result.

* See chapter 30 "Short-sharp-simple"

12 DAYS BEFORE THE BATTLE OF TRAFALGAR,
Admiral Nelson wrote a secret memorandum:
"something must be left to chance; nothing
is sure in a sea fight beyond all others.
In case signals can neither be seen
or perfectly understood, no captain can
do very wrong if he places his ship alongside
that of an enemy."

The rule should be rigid
as in tight rope;
not like an iron bar.
The cord indicates the line,
even when it sags,
and the inflection
does not distort it.
A well-made rule
is both flexible
and straight.

Joseph Joubert (1754-1824)

**Hard and fast rules are there
to be broken, whereas guidelines,
like guide dogs, take you where
you need to go.** Hugh Wilson

19 MANAGING ALONG

I say *"managing along"* because management is, by definition, work in progress. We learn as we go. Managing people is the most difficult task in the world. It's difficult enough trying to manage oneself. Nobody's perfect, neither yourself nor the person you are managing or being managed by.
A recipe for imperfection to the power of two or more.

Management is one of the subjects I have thought about more than any other. My humble bite-sized conclusions are that a) *you should create favourable conditions** b) *that you should clearly explain your values and expectations*, and c) perhaps most importantly, *you should lead through example.*

Nobody tolerates managers who do not practice what they preach. A strong personal moral compass is required and must be kept to. This requires sacrifice. Management is a duty.

If you believe managing your subordinates means sharing your knowledge and inspiring them to achieve better results – then management is a profession. However, if you think management is giving orders and pushing people around, then it is not. Olena Mishakova. Recruitment Expert.

* See chapter 14. *"Favourable conditions"*

I have learnt, the hard way, that however noble one's intentions, management is a never-ending lesson in humility. People from different cultures are very liable to suffer from unintentional misunderstandings. The clashing of culture codes. Having been brought up in England, I was bound to encounter cultural misinterpretations in France. I still do. "Do as you would be done by" doesn't always work.

By telling people where you stand on subjects such as punctuality, initiatives, decision-making, smartphones, etc. you level your playing field and paint the touchlines. The same is true of your boss and their boss . Ask them for their rules. It might avoid the nasty surprise of the odd yellow card later on.

The best management tools are simple. Regular team meetings for open sharing. Honest and routine feedback. Trust and verify.

Animating and motivating

Deciding and Acting

Developing and galvanizing

Being exemplary

The true school of command
is general knowledge.
Charles De Gaulle

You have a duty not to tolerate the poor performer.
Peter Drucker

TO BE IN A POSITION OF POWER, YOU ARE SIGNING UP FOR SACRIFICE.

Jim Collins

I would aim to have more trust in the trustworthy but not in the untrustworthy. In fact, I aim positively to try not to trust the untrustworthy.
We need to focus much more on being trustworthy, and how you give people adequate, useful and simple evidence that you're trustworthy.

Baroness O'Neill. Philosopher.

Pleasure brings performance.
François Gabart. Navigator.

The top motivator of employee performance isn't recognition; it's progress.

Teresa M. Amabile. Professor of Business Administration.

People perform best when they are at play.

Harvard Business Review

It was my job to make sure the team was excellent. Steve Jobs

Workers remain in essence tools in a process in which their own happiness or economic well-being is necessarily incidental. **Alain de Botton. Philosopher.**

Management is manipulation with a smile. Jean Holtzman

"NUNCHI", literally translated, "eye-measure" is the art of sensing what people are thinking and feeling, and responding appropriately. It's speed-reading a room with the emphasis on the collective, not on specific individuals. There is a Korean expression, "Half of social life is Nunchi". The road to hell is paved with empathy. Empathy might be what sets you apart from sociopaths, but it cannot protect you from sociopaths. With excessive empathy, you lose yourself. **Nunchi, by contrast, puts quiet observation first, which allows you to stay on firm ground while still listening to the other person.**

Euny Hong. Korean author.

A culture of trust survives ideas, customers, employees and shareholders. It is the key ingredient for outstanding performance.

Vineet Nayar

People don't need or want to be managed, but to be inspired. A leader is the person who comes up with an idea that galvanizes others.

Vineet Nayar.
Business executive and author.

The manager, who is neither a philosopher nor a social worker, should not waste his time trying to change people, but concentrate on improving their natural skills.

Joan Magretta.
Harvard Business Review contributor.

> To accomplish great things, you must not be above men, but amongst them.
>
> Montesquieu

> My job is to try and create an environment that is best for the players to perform.
>
> Eddie Jones.
> Rugby coach.

> My firm uses a decision-tool called WMKP. It stands for Would my Kids be Proud?
>
> James Atkins.
> Environmental Finance.

> It's not about motivation, it's about trust.
>
> Paul Molga

> Mutual trust is the key to everything.
>
> Nicolas Vanier.
> Husky dog racer.

> Above all, management is knowing how to play down the drama, how to swap the illusion of perfection for a liberating and guilt-free idea: you hobble and limp to manage people.
>
> Frédérick Mispelblom Beyer.
> Professor of Sociology.

> It is much better if players and coach work out their strategy together. Each player participates in the construction of the project and its evaluation. I take the decisions, but they are the result of collective reflection.
>
> Claude Onesta.
> Handball coach.

> Never create a rule that you are not certain you can enforce.
>
> Eric Albert.
> Management Consultant.

Nota Bene: Simple, humble rules and behaviour

FOR YOUR INFORMATION (FYI)

The world has become almost impossibly complex. Business models are changing faster than ever before. And information – true and false, wanted or not – invades our lives 24/7. These three facts of modern life should move brands to organise how both they and their employees bring order to this deluge.

My belief is that it is easier to control information that you methodically and regularly look for, at sources that are both reliable and rich. Quality generalist newspapers, supported by specific publications appropriate to your line of business should suffice. If you methodically " scan " your particular choice of media regularly, then weak signals, early alerts and interesting innovations are to be found on a daily basis.

Information is only useful if it can be easily and quickly summoned to enrich the creative and decision-taking process at will. This requires one's own information to be organised. There are those who believe you can rely on search engines. Useful as web crawlers undoubtedly are, a made-to-measure database should provide a more personal and appropriate answer.

To make good decisions in a complex world, you have to be skilled at ignoring information. Gerd Gigerenzer. Psychologist.

Newspapers: impossible to forgo, but thunder against them!
Flaubert

The most meaningful way to differentiate your company from your competition is to do an outstanding job with information.
How you gather, manage and use information will determine whether you win or lose. Steve Jobs

*THE INFORMATION VIRUS has penetrated us to the very bone, and we are like those alcoholics who wither away as soon as the poison that kills them is removed. It would be so nice not to carry in our heads all the hullabaloo of the century, the head of a man today is so heavy with the appalling heap of things that journalism deposits in it, in such a jumble, every day.
I am well aware that after two or three days one is tired of silence; one becomes anxious, one runs to the train station to buy newspapers. But this is simply proof of the depth of the evil.* Emile Zola. Circa 1900.

We are drowning in information, while starving for wisdom.
Edward Osborne Wilson

Is there anywhere on earth exempt from these swarms of new books? Erasmus (1525)

You always get what you screen for.

Genetic scientist's saying.

The fault I find with NEWSPAPERS is that they force us to take an interest in some fresh TRIVIALITY every day, whereas only three or four books in a lifetime give us anything that is of real importance. Suppose that, every morning, when we tore the wrapper off our paper with fevered hands, a transmutation were to take place, and we were to find inside it - oh! I don't know; shall we say *Pascal's Pensées?* Marcel Proust

FYI Gather knowledge for future action

21 NOTA BENE

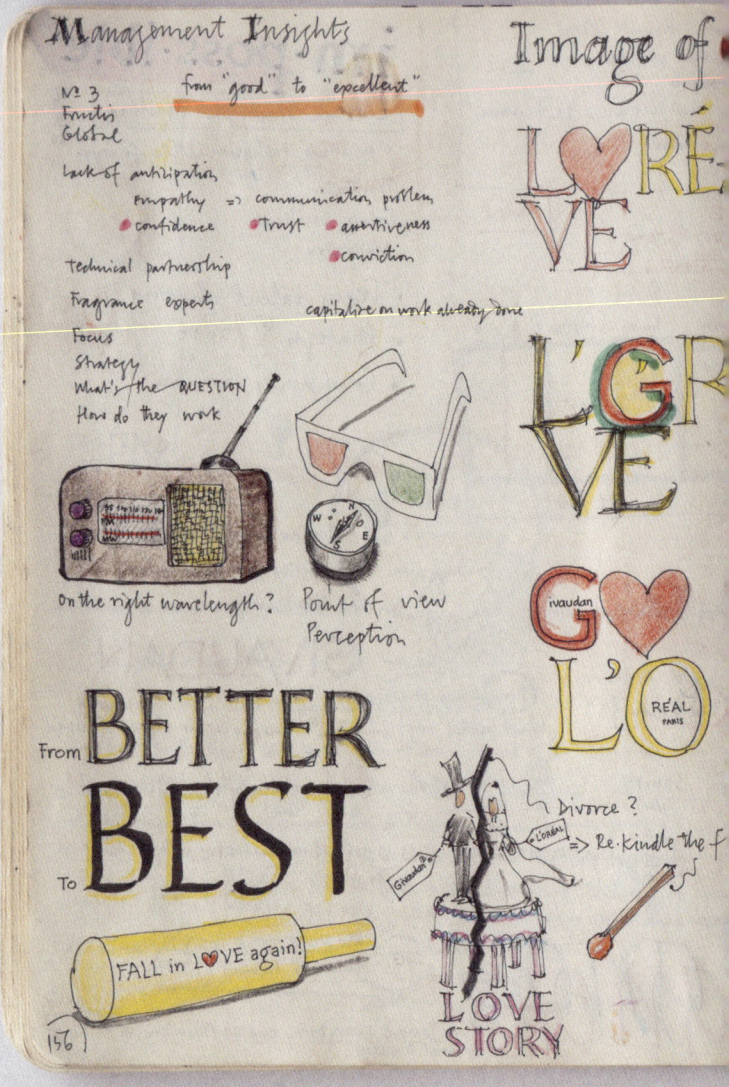

Notes taken by the author during a Givaudan seminar concerning one of their major clients: L'Oréal.

21 NOTA BENE

If we are, as Aristotle said, what we repeatedly do, then I am definitely an enthusiastic, if not obsessive, note-taker. Taking notes, and note, of what people say or write, is surely the easiest way to gradually build one's personal encyclopedia.

Our memories are fickle at best and benefit from not being overcrowded. Notes are therefore allies. Notes enable you to honour, with precision, the sources of information you share. Notes help you to think and to slowly forge opinions. Notes are, as several quotations below attest, vehicles for travelling in time and sources of nostalgic Proustian time-travel pleasures. Reading your own notes procures the pleasant sentiment of déjà vu or to be more precise déjà lu.

Notebooks, notes in books, file cards and filing systems – be they paper or digital – are all aspects of N.ota B.ene. Chronological notes, taken page after page, quietly follow the course of your personal history. The quotations in each chapter of this book come straight from the folders I keep to organise my collection of thoughts. Computers now have integrated search functions that do away with time-consuming analytical classification.

Whether you ever refer to your notes or not, the very making of them assuredly contributes to percolating and stimulating your own thinking.

My notebook allows me to put the world in order.

VADE MECUM - [Go with me]
A compendium containing information about best practices
or techniques or a course of action to be followed,
that is kept to hand for reference.

TRAVELLING IN TIME

"I can time travel, really." He opens the volume of a notebook diary to absorb his writings and sketches and explains that in revisiting his younger self he returns to inhabit the experience of writing and thinking – and feeling - as if time hasn't moved on. Gavin Rookledge. Bookbinder.

> Halfway between creative intuition and reflective thought, the note is a "hybrid form" that retains the liveliness of a poem.
> Monique Petillon

TRACES OF THE READER I ONCE WAS

"I like discovering, in almost forgotten volumes, traces of the reader I once was - scribbles, bus tickets, scraps of paper with mysterious names and numbers, the occasional date and place on the book's flyleaf which take me back to a certain café, a distant hotel room, a far-away summer so long ago." Alberto Manguel

> Unlike cuttlefish, if I spit ink, it's not to protect my escape but to ensure my progress.
> Antoine Emaz. Author.

A FILING SYSTEM IS A CONTROL DEVICE

It submits what is put on a card file to a graphical reasoning that produces coherency, commensurability, sequence, taxonomy and chronology according to the choices made by the person who constitutes it.
It imposes rationality on the disorder of the world and on the disorder of words and things. This appropriation of the world and this desire for control manifest themselves in the choice of a principle of order.
Jean-François Bert

EVERYTHING I HAVE EVER READ

For Joseph Jacobson, professor at the Massachusetts Institute of Technology (MIT), the last, the ultimate book would be a compendium that would contain not only all the texts he had ever read, including his annotations in the margins, but also all his notes on his inventions and ideas. "A book that would accompany me for the rest of my life."

The author offers us line spacing and margins, so you can write your thoughts in between his.
Jean Guitton

JOURNALING

Scientific studies have shown the benefits of journaling, like an increase in mindfulness, memory and communication skills, better sleep, a stronger immune system, more self-confidence and a higher IQ. Hayley Phelan.

Logically, pinboards should replace museums.
John Berger (1972)

MENTAL GYMNASTICS

Thinking with file cards and a filing system, is to engender intellectual operations of serialization, of linking, by showing oneself capable of creating semantic similarities, analogies, variations, differences, continuities and discontinuities. It also means practising mental gymnastics that allow one to focus attention on the particular case as well as on the whole series into which the singular is inserted. In short, it is to operate changes of scale, from the whole to the part and vice versa.

Jean-François Bert

IT FEELS LIKE THINKING

There's a fundamental difference between searching a universe of documents created by strangers and searching your own personal library. When you're freewheeling through ideas that you yourself have collated – particularly when you'd long ago forgotten about them – there's something about the experience that seems uncannily like freewheeling through the corridors of your own memory. It feels like thinking.
Steven Berlin Johnson

THAT VOLUME AND NO OTHER

The volume I hold in my hands, that volume and no other, becomes the Book. Annotations, stains, marks of one kind or another, a certain moment and place, characterize that volume as surely as if it were a priceless manuscript.
Alberto Manguel

Nowadays, 90% of my inspiration comes from internet. I keep everything on my hard drive. Pictures, words... I store everything in my 4,000 or so folders.
When I'm looking for inspiration, I go for a search on MY CLOUD.
Peter Saville. Graphic Designer.

When gazing at a tree or a fire,
you don't think about taking notes.
Christian Bobin

I forget who it was who said that
every author should keep
a NOTEBOOK, but should take care
NEVER TO REFER TO IT.
If you understand this properly,
I think there is truth in it.
Somerset Maugham

The way to learn is to re-read a lot. I could not list all of the treasures and precious remarks which I have discovered in familiar books, those that I have read twenty times over and which have enlightened me. I could not make an inventory of all those treasures; I know them not. I do not write them down; if I knew them, IF I WROTE THEM DOWN, IT WOULD BE DEAD KNOWLEDGE.
It is a noble art, in my opinion, and too often ignored, to read without wanting to learn, simply to distract oneself. Those readings become incorporated; they nourish and relax. They are the perfect remedy to all that file card knowledge, that one cannot do without completely, but which only ever remains on the surface. Alain. Philosopher.

University notes taken by the author in the 1980's.

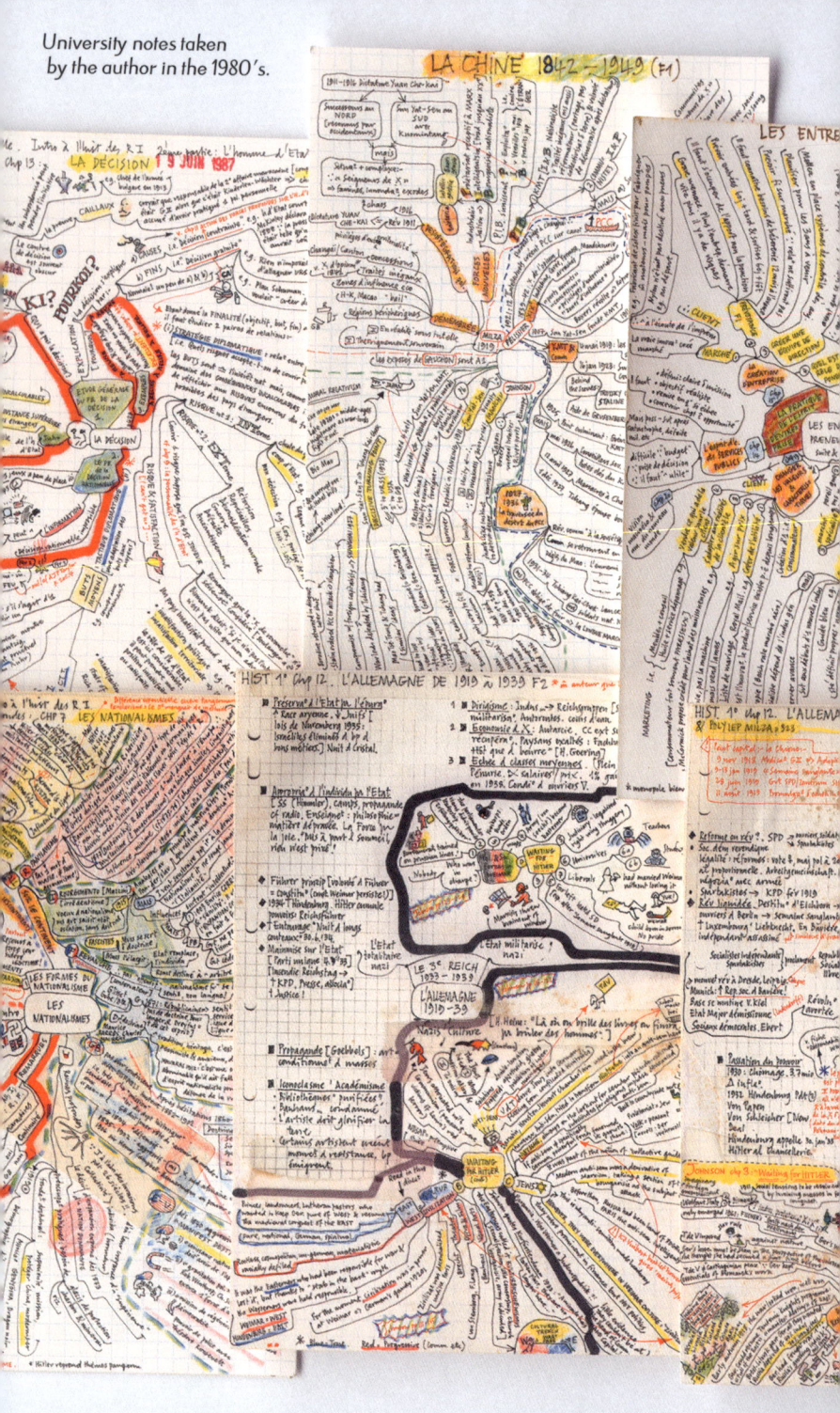

The cheeky garbage of an active mind.
William.L.Hamilton on Shinro Ohtake's scrapbooks.

Basquiat was a creator of lists. He would write down words, names, facts, diagrams from varied scientific domains: anatomy, geography, chemistry, alchemy, cartography, history, history of art, books, Bibles, encyclopedias, dictionaries…these sources become MATERIAL THAT BRING THE WHOLE WORLD INTO HIS PAINTINGS.
Basquiat exhibition. Louis Vuitton foundation. 2018.

Message in a bottle
Bottling ideas in files and folders
Forget-me-not
Keys to who knows what
Lifelong lifelines
Treasure chest

N.B. Create an efficient and personal encyclopedia

22 STIMULATING IDEAS

IDEAS ARE LIKE LIGHT BULBS.
They only work if you insert them into a live socket. Ideas have to be given to people in such a way that they immediately light up in their minds. They have to make sense and make contact.

There is a beautiful phrase in the Saint James version of the Bible: "wisdom crieth without". You never quite know when, or from whom, you might hear, read or witness wisdom crying out to you. You should perhaps also listen to yourself, for methinks "wisdom crieth within".

To mix two contemporary metaphors, I see ideas like spheres in a pinball machine, bouncing off people and random readings. From time to time you might just see yourself in other people's ideas: "idea-selfies" of sorts.

> The problem is not to come up with ideas, but to find out which one is worth the time.
> Ron Arad. Designer.

WISDOM CRIETH *WITHOUT*
WISDOM CRIETH *WITHIN*

Ideas fade into view.
Steven Berlin Johnson. Author and journalist.

The question reveals the answer.
Christian Bobin. Author.

A thought is something as real as a cannonball.
Joseph Joubert

Madam, I never have new ideas.
Cristobal Balenciaga. Couturier.

What's the idea?
Philippe Michel. Adman.

In Greek, "*idea*" derives from "*I saw*".
Chema Madoz. Photographer.

Fuel the idea.
Freddo freelance cameraman, Irancy, Burgundy.

Ideas come from everything, from everywhere.
David Lynch. Artist and Film Director.

I've always pursued an idea that ends up differently.
Georg Baselitz. Artist.

**A good creative idea,
is the one that scares me.**
John Hegarty. Adman.

What is a new, brilliant and extraordinary thought?

It is not, as the ignorant persuade themselves, a thought that no one has ever had, nor should have had.

On the contrary, it is a thought that has occurred to everyone but which someone is the first to express.

A fine expression says something that everyone has thought, only says it in a lively, fine and new manner.

Nicolas Boileau. French poet. 1636-1711.

The unearthing of ideas. That is what design is all about. The rest is just layout. Alan Fletcher. Graphic Designer.

An idea that is not dangerous is unworthy of being called an idea at all. Oscar Wilde

Ideas are in the air. All it takes is for someone to talk about them from close up and you'll catch them.

Raymond Devos. French comedian.

Ideas are the easiest thing to come up with. Just read or watch science fiction. I'm a big fan. It's all there already, you just have to be crazy enough to try to make it real.

Palmer Luckey.
Founder of Oculus Rift
Virtual Reality Headsets.

Where is the idea? You cannot invent ideas; you have to look for them where they are.

Alain. Pseudonym of Émile-Auguste Chartier. Philosopher.

I. D. Stimulating ideas energize

NIGHTHINKING

Waking up with ideas is a common phenomenon.

It is therefore strange that few people turn this possibility into a technique, even if many famous creators admit that ideas come to them upon awakening: Karl Lagerfeld, Marc Newson, Ray Bradbury, Paul McCartney, Helmut Newton and Jean Nouvel to mention but a few. Recently science has proven that during the night the brain reorganises thoughts from the day before.

They say you shouldn't disturb a good night's sleep with a late afternoon siesta. But I once had a nap after work to recharge my batteries for the evening and woke up twenty minutes later with ideas pulsating around my brain...

Having pencil and pad beside your bed is a must.

However, if the notebook is too small you might, as I discovered one morning, be unable to read what you scribbled in the dark. I also discovered that I can wake up exactly on time by gently hitting my pillow with my head the number of times that corresponds to the desired wake-up hour.

It's as if sleep were a corridor to my imagination.
Eric-Emmanuel Schmitt

> **I find going to bed and pulling my imagination over my head often means waking up with a solution to a design problem.**
>
> Alan Fletcher

Taking an hour-long photograph at night with a large format camera is both amusing and instructive. The slow-time-long-exposure allows the light-in-the-dark to gently seep in through the lens and onto the film. Is there a link between seep in and sleep in? Perhaps if one were to consider one's brain at night like the sensitive recording device it is, one might be able to develop those thought rays in the morning. No flash, just time. Night time. The brain needs time to think: load it with film early every morning and leave it on shutter release mode at night.

> **I go to sleep to come up with my ideas.**
> **I get a lot of my ideas from lucid dreaming.**
> **I've taught myself to wake up to write them down.**
>
> Daniel Lismore

> *Monks have the custom, as old as piety itself, of sowing their subject of meditation, like a seed, in the furrows of the night. They hope upon waking to find the seed already softened, penetrated by the humidity of the earth and perhaps even germinated; it will grow even more quickly in the sunbeams of reflection and grace.*
>
> **A.D. Sertillanges**

Eureka : Practice using your subconscious

CREATIVE CONSTRAINTS

Clear constraints are what brands should give their creative partners. If every brief started by stating the constraints; everybody would gain in terms of creativity, speed, enjoyment and results. The magazine *i-D* is a perfect example : the model on the cover systematically winks and has done since 1980.

The metaphor of a deep narrow canyon, like the Colorado, bouncing kayaks down its gorge illustrates well the power of tight constraints. The placid meander of the Loire valley, on the contrary, lacks both speed and specific direction.

> Constraints liberate you
> and bring the only freedom that matters.
> Antoine de Saint-Exupéry

Saint Cloud is more beautiful than Versailles, because the slope of the land directed the gardener's thoughts. Alain. Philosopher.

The constraint of choosing to shoot a photograph today with either analogue film, or in black and white, or exclusively in large format would quickly narrow down the choice of photographers for a start.

Art is born of constraints, lives from struggles and dies of freedom.
André Gide

At the 2014 show we had at Alcatraz, you couldn't touch the prison walls, you couldn't hang anything. It was really strict, but I think freedom comes from those restrictions. Ai Weiwei

Without constraints we would be lost. Even if it means overstepping them sometimes. Renzo Piano. Architect.

The very first time Nick Knight shot Isabella Rossellini for a Lancôme Make Up colour story, he used what he called his " washing machine ": an 8" x 10 " camera loaded with Polaroids. Isabella admitted having never before been photographed with such a slow process camera. Even if towards the end of the day's shooting, Nick Knight hedged his bets with some rolls of medium format 6x6 film, I am pleased to say that we chose to use one of the 8x10 Polaroids on account, amongst other things, of their inimitably beautiful subtle colours.

A river hampered by narrow banks surges forwards.
A.D. Sertillanges. Philosopher.

Life is never stronger than when it is thwarted on one side, impeded in its direction: it flows freely through the opening that remains. Christian Bobin. Author.

CREATIVE GRID CONSTRAINTS

The layout of this book follows the grid below.
We admit on occasion to have taken slight artistic liberties
as frameworks are guidelines, not straightjackets.

Why this grid?

The nine-division construction stems from the golden
section and has been used since Greek times by scribes
and monks. Fitting therefore that a " brand bible "
take its secular proportions from divine inspiration
and exemplars. The grid offers both innumerable
paragraph combinations to better underline sense,
whilst ensuring a unified design sequence.

Mathematical ratios are however only a starting point.
In practice the eye and critical judgement have
the final say. Each graphic designer, or brand, develop
their idiosyncratic rule-of-thumb that should
be as singular as their own handwriting.

We chose a page format of 11.8 x 17.8 cm : large enough
to be attractive and small enough to be practical.
Margins abound for notes and glosses.

Why these typefaces?

As debated in chapter 12, there is only a fine line
between fonts. Axel Vagnard created ONION TYPE
DESIGN (OTD + OTD italic) specifically for this book

Learn more on OTD on page 266/267.

PAGE NUMBER	BOOK'S TITLE	NUMBER OF CHAPTER + NAME
156	A BRAND IS AN ONION	24 - CREATIVE CONSTRAINTS

in 2019 and **we chose AKZIDENZ GROTESK, designed by the Berthold Type Foundry of Berlin in 1896, to be its partner**.

OTD is used for the body of text, with Akzidenz's natural strength and simplicity being the perfect foil. In a quest for balance, variety and elation, we have played with upper and lower-case letters, italics, font size and colour in order to limit the number of fonts to just two.

Why these colours?

Black and grey [50% & 20%] enable the author to speak, whisper and nudge. They are moreover a pleasant reminiscence of Kodak grey scale cards. Red and blue are on both the Union Jack and the Tricolour. The CMJN blue contains inimitable Cyanotype undertones whilst the hard-hitting red keeps the reader awake.

I have also just realised, perhaps unconscious serendipity [?], that the below colours are also those of the brands I have worked for (Lancôme, Givaudan, Clarins; Handmade).

I WANT THE ARTIST IN CHAINS, BUT I WANT HIM TO BE A LION.

Freedom is counterproductive for artists. Their genius needs a sort of prison, like a boiler generating steam. I would recommend that a wicked tyrant give them a wall to decorate, or an arch to sculpt; or have a block of marble brought to a sculptor with the injunction to carve somebody's portrait. It is to be remarked that since time immemorial the portrait has probably been the subject of the most powerful works of art; it is because the model becomes a tyrant. It seems to me that the more freedom is thwarted, the more it asserts itself; its claws mark better in a resistant material. Shakespeare wrote for his troupe, and so did Molière. I want the artist in chains, but I want him to be a lion. **Alain. Philosopher.**

When I published a small notebook for my clients as a gift, I gave myself the constraint of using a light bulb to convey the idea of ideas. I was pleased when I discovered that black light bulbs – with a hint of violet - actually exist.
Black on black: perhaps a metaphor for the creative process of fumbling for ideas in the dark.

The raw material determines the shape.
Alain

A commission is a clamp.
Edmonde Charles-Roux. Author.

I can only write under constraints, under the pressure of joy.
Christian Bobin. Author.

The chisel guides the artist's hand.
Alain. Philosopher

We're always free in a frame.
Stéphane Ridel. Film maker.

Spirit in a bottle.
Joseph Joubert. Thinker

Constraints increase creative potential.
Alan Fletcher. Designer.

The raw material is our guide.
René Pechère. Garden Designer.

My experience with HAND**MADE**™ **corroborates**
the philosopher Alain's theory of the importance of raw
materials and how the more a texture "resists" the better.
I took a series of photos of different ingredients in the
shape of the Union Jack, using a cardboard template to
ensure coherence. As can be seen below, the wobbly 3-D
strawberry jelly was far more delicate to manoeuvre into
place than the raspberry jam that I simply spread into shape
with a spoon. The natural resistance of the jelly
led to a far more interesting photograph.

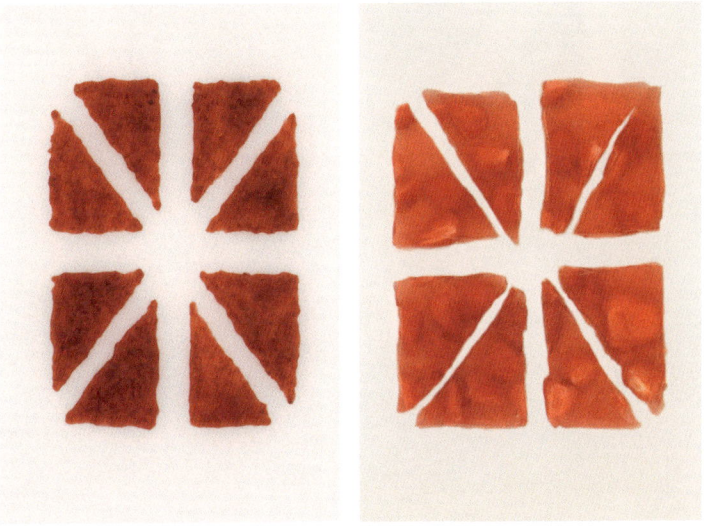

C-à-d : Giving carte blanche generates a black hole

25 BRANDING IS ABOUT

CREA

TIVITY

BRANDING IS ABOUT CREATIVITY

Creativity is the very lifeblood of brands. Recently its importance has been better acknowledged and certain Art Directors [cf Apple, Burberry, Dior etc.] have been given decision-making power that would have been unheard of only a few years ago. Indeed, most multinational marketing groups recruit graduates from business schools, who often proudly [and mistakenly] declare that they have no creative talent. I've never quite understood why all children are encouraged to be polymaths in kindergarten and are just as happy - and proficient - playing with paint, numbers and words; but as young men (perhaps this is especially true in France, where mathematics is the " royal road ") they look upon paint and wordplay as a job solely reserved for " creative " people.

Creativity is both an attitude and an action. Being *and* **doing.**

Being, *in a state of expectant joy, open to folly and to the absurd, whilst listening to your instincts and following your hunches. Lucid dream-thinking, if you will.*

Doing, in a particular place, over possibly a long stretch of time. Doing is also watching, observing, scanning, dredging and panning. Writing on paper is apparently an action that stimulates seven different zones of the brain. Drawing creates images, encourages mental drift, as does walking – that supposedly increases creativity by 80%. Doing is questioning and connecting unexpected things, people and ideas.

In short, creation is hard work and a flexible mind. The art of looking sideways, to coin Alan Fletcher's title. A transformation. A disruption?

Try changing the shape of your mind. You can even think like somebody else, if you try. From everything that I have seen, heard or read about the designer Philippe Starck it would appear that his way of thinking involves a mixture of humour, distance, and candour. When I ask my students to think like Philippe Starck and then imagine what he created for two small projects that I followed closely, they always succeed in guessing correctly.

Creativity is at the heart of Branding and therefore the main topic of this book.

Creation comes from ordinary acts. **This does not make creating easy. Magic is instant, genius an accident of birth.** Take them away & what is left is work. Work is the soul of creation.

Kevin Ashton

We design *in the morning,* **we make** *in the afternoon,* **and we fail** *in the evening.*

Will Jackson. Robot constructor.

Try again. Fail again. Fail better. Samuel Beckett

You don't really see something unless you draw it. Alan Fletcher

tions
s no
ula.

I make things to experience the process. Kiki Smith. Artist.

I place a sheet of white paper on the table and wait for the words, attracted by the light, to be caught on it. Christian Bobin

Charlotte Perriand

If you know where an idea comes from and why, *it's marketing.*

Karl Lagerfeld

It is not so much a question of «*thinking out of the box***» as they say, but of «***thinking the box***», *opening it up to novelty,* and *redefining its contours.***

Etienne Candel. Researcher CNRS.

« **LA** QUESTION **ÉVEILLE LA** *RÉPONSE* ».

The question *awakens* the answer.
The question *arouses* the answer.
The question *prompts* the answer.
The question *triggers* the answer.
The question *provokes* the answer.
The question *sparks* the answer.
The question *generates* the answer.
The question *reveals* the answer.
The question *elicits* the answer.
Christian Bobin

This underlines the importance of a good brief.

Make, *break*, make, *break*.
James Dyson

IN ORDER TO THINK-INVENT, THERE'S NO NEED TO BE SERIOUS, AUSTERE OR ABSTRACT. THAT WOULD BE COUNTERPRODUCTIVE. IT IS BETTER TO ABANDON ONESELF, TO LET ONESELF BE CARRIED ALONG, TO PLUNGE INTO THE FLOW, TO BECOME A BEAR, A FOX, A BEAVER, A TREE OR A TORRENT – EITHER IN TURN, OR ALL TOGETHER –, TO RELY ON THE BIFURCATIONS THAT ARE OFFERED. ALWAYS PREFER IMBALANCE AND ASYMMETRY, WHICH ARE THE ONLY WAYS FORWARD. ERROR, DEVIANCE, MONSTROSITY, THESE ARE THE FIRST ACTORS OF ANY CREATION. Roger-Pol Droit

FAUSSE BONNE IDÉE. FALSE-GOOD-IDEA.

The French have a widely used expression: "*fausse bonne idée*". Literally "false good idea". The mere fact that the phrase exists must underline just how often a good idea reveals itself to be a bad one. And vice versa.

Hugh Wilson

creation is a continuous mistake!
paco rabanne.

Solvitur ambulando.
[It is solved by walking]

creativity is not about seducing people, but about shocking them.
paco rabanne

I have walked myself into my best thoughts.
Kierkegaard.
Philosopher.

Every place of retirement requires a walk. My thoughts fall asleep if I seat them. My mind will not move, if my legs do not stir it.
Michel de Montaigne

A routine creates a landing place for the muse.
Alex Soojung-Kim Pang

Total Rep

> Every **mistake pays off** BECAUSE I can use it as **a fresh start.**
> Anselm KIEFER, Artist.

> Every act of creation is above all an act of destruction.
> **Pablo Picasso**

> **A good creative idea is one that scares me.**
> John Hegarty. Adman.

fail.

Creativity is just connecting things.
Steve Jobs

eat. *Linda Rubright*

It takes a moment of delirium to create.
Louis-Ferdinand Céline

Try again. Fail again. Fail better.
Samuel Beckett

To sum up: Net sales follow creative actions

26 YET THERE IS METHOD IN IT

To be, or not to be methodical? Two schools confront each other concerning methods. And, as often, the answer probably lies in the middle, in the difficult and delicate balance. As George Orwell in his sixth and last rule on writing says: " break any of these rules sooner than say anything outright barbarous." (cf p. 215)

I have learnt in practice, that if you do have some sort of a method, you can then use it, change it or drop it, depending on the situation. Descartes believed that problems need to be divided into manageable sizes. Breaking jobs down into stages is the role of a plan and a timetable. Checklists avoid unnecessary frustrations. Jet fighter pilots scrupulously follow their aircraft manual until they are airborne. Then they can concentrate on their real savoir-faire and natural talent, which is to fly and wage war.

The phase of forward-thinking and retro-planning also reduces stress which is directly linked to not having put aside sufficient time for the job in hand.

I like to imagine carpenters and masons of bygone ages building houses whilst simply measuring with their thumbs and feet. To create your own professional thumb rules strikes me as the balanced attitude to adopt. Joseph Joubert's beautiful metaphor of string rules being more suitable than those made of iron gives practical and sensible C17th French guidelines for modern management.

Divide each of the difficulties under examination into as many parts as possible, and as might be necessary for its adequate solution. Descartes

One thing at a time,
and done very well;
is a very good rule,
as many can tell.
English nursery rhyme

Carving the subject at its natural joints. Aristotle.

The most valuable truths are methods. Nietzsche

Talent without technique is but mannerism.
Georges Brassens. Singer, song-writer and poet.

The answer is in the room.

Intuition and instinct
are the only things we know for sure.
Hiro. Photographer.

In Chinese, Korean or Japanese, the tens are separated by saying, for example, ten and one, ten and two. This «language factor» allows children to break down numbers and thus count faster mentally. Brigitte Perucca. CNRS.
[French National Centre for Research]

Paul Auster works *without a plan, chiselling one sentence after the other, "walking onwards to the last one"*.

Florence Noiville. Author and journalist.

FIRST OR SECOND INSTINCTS?

Our first instincts are often right, but when we start to have second thoughts, the second thoughts are usually occurring for a reason. It is better to switch. The lesson is that if you are hesitating over whether to leave things as they are, you probably needed to make a change some time ago.

Tim Harford. Journalist and author.

You can learn techniques in a workshop,
but art is something you have to bring yourself.
Markus Lüpertz. German Painter.

**The term «method», in itself, I find repellent.
The actor's wealth is his imagination.** Denis Lavant. Actor.

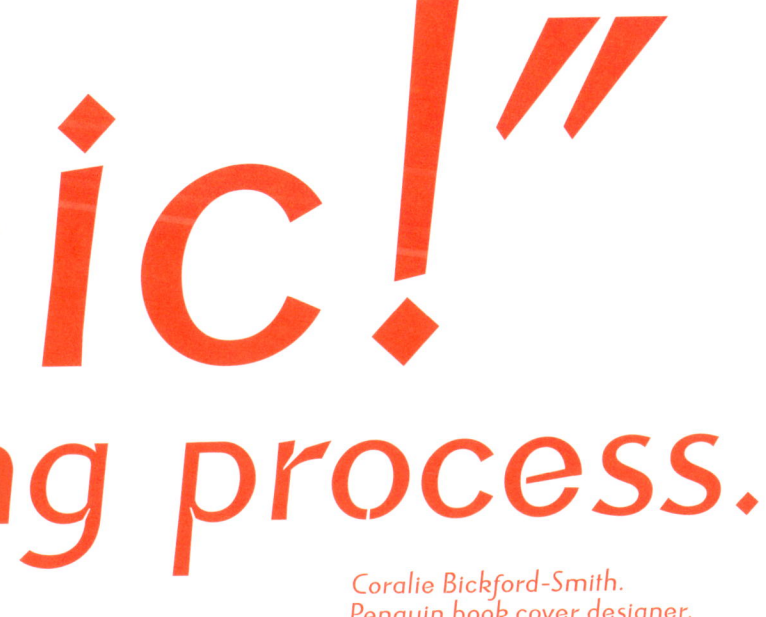

*Coralie Bickford-Smith.
Penguin book cover designer.*

**There is a form for everyone's thinking,
which must be found; *but not sought*.**
Alain. Pseudonym of Émile-Auguste Chartier. Philosopher.

Sometimes when I can't think of what to do,
I wonder *" what would Irving Penn do?"*,
but I can't imagine what Penn would do,
because he would never do what one expected.
Phyllis Poswick. Executive Fashion Editor of Vogue.

AS IF YOU WERE...

If biographies of famous leaders are so popular with business people, it is probably because you can learn from the example of famous people just as easily as from teachers, mentors and colleagues.

Philippe Starck, the world-famous French designer has a very straightforward creative technique that can easily be copied, if not reproduced. Starck's attitude is often a mixture of cliché, common knowledge and humour. He was once asked to redesign the cover of a famous French editor's encyclopedia. The editor in question is called Larousse, which sounds identical to the French words "la rousse" : 'the redheaded girl'. Needless to say, the cover he proposed for Larousse was a photo of a ginger-haired girl. He adopted the same straightforward tongue-in-cheek attitude when working on an aborted perfume project for Lancôme. The code name for the perfume was "idleness"; so he duly designed a bottle with a glass cushion as a rest.

Just follow the stringline.
René Jodelet. Blacksmith.

George Prêtre, the 80-year-old conductor says that every time he takes a score, he looks at it AS IF IT WERE the very first time. Hence, he says, his youthful spirit.
Jacques Chancel. Journalist.

René Jodelet is a blacksmith in Burgundy who has hammered, twisted and forged more than ten tons of iron for my garden. He has his recurrent words of wisdom I enjoy hearing. "On demand"* is his favourite. It means that each piece of iron will naturally be worked and placed according to what the last piece of iron "demands". A superb craftsman with an ultra-practical mind-set. I took this photo of him in his workshop. Vulcan in his forge.   *"À la demande".

P.P.S. Mastering a certain degree of technique is essential

26 I.C.E.
YET THERE IS METHOD IN IT

INSPIRATION CON·

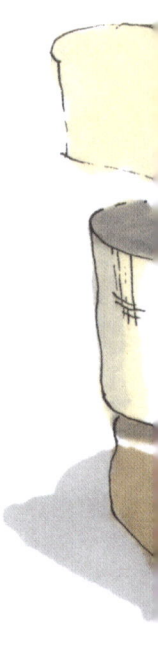

My sketch above is a poor substitute for Irving Penn's "Italian Still Life (A)". Unfortunately the Irving Penn Foundation refused me permission to use his photo. But I nevertheless thank them kindly for having replied to my request, stating: "a drawing based on Mr Penn's photograph is fine". I hope you agree...

EXECUTION

This simple three-step method is fairly universal. It doesn't always work in the above order. Execution can bring Inspiration.

ON SEEING AND LOOKING

There is a book on the wonderful early C20th German portrait photographer August Sander entitled: "Seeing, Observing and Thinking". This title underlines the importance of looking – with care – to the creative process.

In every object there is inexhaustible meaning; the eye sees in it what the eye brings means of seeing. Thomas Carlyle

My weapon is the way I look at my era.
Yves Saint Laurent

Sight is the mind's touch. Pessoa

I don't necessarily want to show something to you, the viewers. Rather I want to allow myself to see what things are. Guido Guidi. Photographer.

Our sight nourishes 85% of our feelings.
Paul Reps. American poet.

Today the eye is the prince of the world. Joseph Delteil. French poet.

Some people know how to look, but others can't even see. Nadar. C19th French photographer.

I can become obsessed with anything... if I look at it long enough. That's the photographer's curse. Irving Penn. Photographer.

Seeing is equivalent to knowing, thinking and also understanding. It is with this intuitive insight that I create. Takenobu Igarashi. Japanese designer.

One can travel the world and see nothing. To achieve understanding it is necessary not to see many things but to look hard at what you do see. Giorgio Morandi

The thrill of seeing. Nicolas Fox-Weber. Art historian.

SEE WITHOUT THINKING

The important thing is that we know how to see,
    To see without thinking,
    To see when you see
    And not to think when you see
    Nor see when you think.

Pessoa

Videlicit Look hard, often and again

LEARNING TO LOOK

Everything is beautiful, if you know how to look. But you have to learn to look. We get used to looking just as we get used to carrying a burden. Thus the sight of familiar things no longer awakens us. Alain. French philosopher.

Let me see.
Charles Dickens

Where you look is where you go.
Motorbike riding instructor

We look at *things*.
The Japanese, they look
at *the space between* things.
Pierre Charpin. French designer.

Keep your eyes as wide open as a paper fan.
Charlotte Perriand

To see, you don't have to know anything except how to see.
Wols. German painter.

One never knows well what one has not seen.
Alain. French Philosopher.

Look, see, observe...
Stare
Behold
Contemplate
View
Notice
Consider
Study
Watch
Admire
Eye
Detect
Scan
Search
Examine
Inspect
Scrutinize
Perceive
Discern

28 FLASHES *IN FRAGMENTS*

"Licks and scrapes". One of my first childhood memories, was of being allowed to lick and scrape the fruitcake bowl, before the cake was put in the oven. Over and above the forbidden pleasure of eating uncooked cake mix, it was perhaps also, as Malcolm Gladwell suggests in his book *Blink*, an early experience of "thinslicing": of how a fragment of something can give you a clear - and enjoyable - idea of the whole.

Pareto's 20/80 law of the vital few is perhaps more serious proof for my belief in quotations and rules of thumb. After all, the Ten Commandments are probably more useful to Jews and Christians than the 800,000-odd words of the Old Testament.

There are those, and I am in fairly good company here, who can only think and write in leaps and bounds.
The classical French thinkers Montaigne and Joseph Joubert and the contemporary writer Patrick Modiano have all admitted to being structurally piecemeal.
Voltaire famously warned that the surest way to bore people is to tell them everything. So perhaps fragments and snippets could be likened to sparks that help light blazes of thought.

The most useful thoughts are those that give help when you need it. Such ideas are rarely long philosophical essays, but more probably a conviction or opinion that helps you better understand a situation or make a decision.

And the most useful rules of thumb are those that are easily shared. Nowadays people talk of memes, whose main quality is that of being easily memorable.

Long before notification-interruptions diminished people's attention span to roughly that of a goldfish, my motto has been to try and keep things short-sharp-and-simple. Packaging ideas into convenient bite-sized morsels is precisely the strength and appeal of proverbs, quotations, maxims and Haikus.

I trust that you, the reader of *A Brand is an Onion*, will agree with a student who once said that my lectures were *"fragments that form a whole"*.

I write only in small snippets, small thoughts, small wounds, that can put me in a situation where I'm sharing with or consoling the reader. Ornela Vorpsi. Albanian writer and photographer.

> The significance of Marcel Proust's work lies in each fragment.
> The book can be opened wherever one wishes; its vitality does not depend on what goes before. Paul Valéry

Kurz gesagt Fragments are easy to share and to remember

Our vision of the world comes through fragments,

I confess to being a butterfly of Parnassus. I am lightheartedly fickle and fly from flower to flower and from subject to subject.
Jean de La Fontaine

Scattered notes with no sequel, like dreams, like life that is made up of various pieces and many collaborations.
Paul Gauguin

through the rhythm of emotions

We do not keep in our memory homogeneous books, but mingled fragments torn from partial readings, and further remodelled by our personal fantasies: snippets of falsified books.

Pierre Bayard. Professor at the Sorbonne.

and feelings.

Alain Kervern. Author of Haikus.

Non sequitur

Bits and bobs

Snippets and titbits

Slivers, shavings and shreds

Flying-thought catcher

Nuggets

Juxtapositions

Wild leaps
and abrupt jumps

Stimulating thinking

29 PICTURE THINKING©

I believe so strongly in the creative-catalyst-power of images that I even registered this compound word as a brand, back in the Noughties. Roland Barthes endorses my conviction when he includes three plurals in the phrase:
" images create desires for ideas "
Ideas don't necessarily always appear through images, but images definitely stimulate the synapses.

Perhaps the best example of how I believe Picture-Thinking functions is to tell the story of the creative process of my Picture-Thinking© logo. I had always considered myself something of a dab hand at visualizing a photographic concept, good at representing it through a doodle-brief in order to have it then shot by a professional photographer. This is the very subject of my chapter on METHODS. Seeing as I was working on my very own logo, I therefore spent more time than usual in carefully thinking through the project [*which might just explain why the process was methodically chaotic*].

> A drawing that is too precise is an obstacle to the freedom to create, it should not be a straitjacket, just an impulse. *The important thing is the idea.*
> Jean Nouvel

To illustrate the words Picture-Thinking, I toyed with dozens of ideas ranging from light bulbs to cartoon-thought-bubbles, but finally decided to shoot a walnut in a half open shell, a metaphor for an open mind.

Everything went according to plan until the day of the shoot. I arrived at the studio with a kilo of walnuts and a nutcracker, in order to remove the top half of a nutshell. Try as I might, the nutshells all broke in strange places and not one single trial gave me the " Fabergé egg " look I had thought would be the easiest of tasks. The best I could do was extract an unbroken walnut from its shell. As I was miles from the nearest " walnut shop " and had rented the studio for the day, I decided to at least shoot the walnut - without its shell. Being an obedient slave to a professional trick I had learnt in the cosmetic industry, I doubled the first colour Polaroid with a 4x5 black and white one, in order to check the sharpness of the focus on the mythical " 55 " Polaroid peel-apart negative, before shooting the definitive Ektachrome film.

Whereas the colour Polaroid of the walnut, five minutes earlier, had depressed me by its banal reality, the negative of the same naked walnut revealed what looked to me like an eerie, blue " brain " on a black background. I had been trying to photograph a metaphor for thought and all of a sudden here was the closest one could get to a picture of a brain without dissecting a skull. The final logo cuts the positive and negative in equal halves: is it the picture of a nut or a brain?
Both. Picture-Thinking, in a nutshell. Or rather without one.

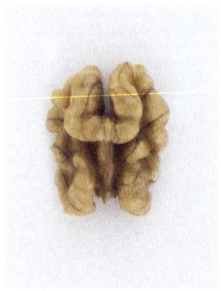 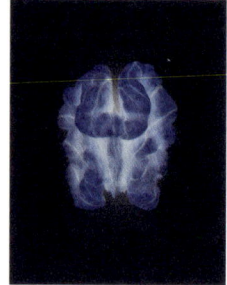

EPILOGUE. Of course the next time I cracked open a walnut to accompany a glass of Chablis, lo and behold, there was my doodle-drawing. I took a photo with my smartphone and thanked the God of nuts and nutcrackers that my initial idea had been thwarted by reality, only to be changed through picture-thinking.

> *An image is naked
> if it is not supported by a word.*
> Roman Cieslewicz

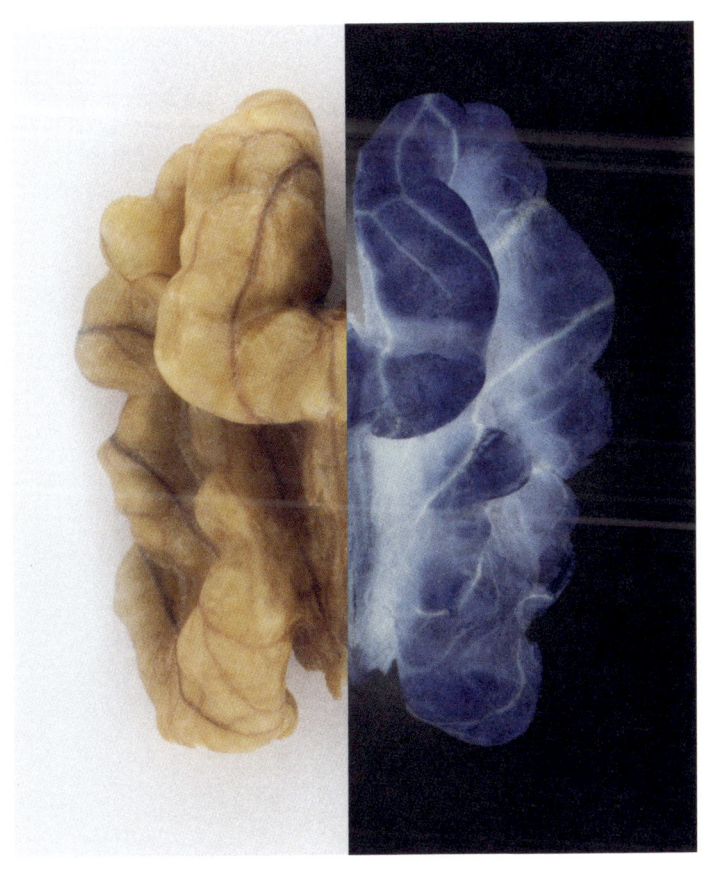

PICTURE THINKING©
ideas made visible

TO KNOW IS TO SEE.
TO THINK IS TO LOOK.

To think is to discern. Much more than images or metaphors, these formulas will never cease to stress that philosophy is an ophthalmology – a knowledge of the eye, a history of vision, of direction of the gaze, of accommodation.
The gaze of the other will, for Sartre, transform the subject into a thing. Whatever the era, sight remains for philosophers the imperial sense. This is why the history of Western reasoning is an optical affair: *seeing and thinking endlessly refer back one to the other.* **Roger-Pol Droit. Philosopher.**

Great poets are incredible triggers of images, their words are essential to me, they stimulate me, they open the doors of my imagination. **Francis Bacon. Painter.**

" And what is the use of a book, " thought Alice, " without pictures or conversation? " **Lewis Carroll**

My images have the same function as poetry: awakening. Roman Cieslewicz

VISUALIZING THINGS

I need to visualize things that lead me to other forms, that lead me to visualize forms that lead me to other forms or subjects, details, images that influence my nervous system and transform the basic idea.
Francis Bacon. Painter.

Look with your mind's eye. Hugh Wilson

Unless we can visualize something, we are unable to think about it.

Language can be heard but thought can be seen.
Saint Augustine

I shut my eyes in order to see.
Paul Gauguin

Turner could paint with his eyes open.
Monet

Alan Fletcher

Viz. Make ideas visible

30

SHORT SH

RP SIMPLE

SHORT - SHARP - SIMPLE

A Brand should be simple. Simple to understand. Simple to describe. Simple to sell and simple to buy. The only problem with simple, is that oversimplification is never far away. It is perhaps therefore useful to think of simple as always being linked to two other words beginning with S: short and sharp. I actually spent quite a long, laborious time ruminating on the association of these three words. Short implies having worked hard to abridge. Sweet instead of sharp won't do. Sharp maintains that edge against superficiality. The final result will probably be sweet though.

Simplicity is about subtracting the obvious, and adding the meaningful. John Maeda

People have a naturally tendency to shorten and simplify words. Initials are often preferred over names (LVMH / SNCF etc.). These abbreviations are perhaps perceived as sharper, to prove my three-word-point. One theory has it that the word " nylon " was created by two chemists on a flight from New York to London using the abbreviations on their luggage labels. [NY/LON].

The universal *elevator pitch*, the Japanese *Pecha Kucha* presentations (6 minutes 40 seconds : 20 slides X 20 seconds) or the Australian "*Three Minute Thesis*" [3MT] show the global and growing popularity of brevity.

Images obey the same "short-sharp-simple" rule too. The adman John Hegarty considers the Christian cross as the most symbolic logo ever created. The Swiss and English flags are probably close runners-up, unless the red Japanese circle pips them to the flagpole as being even shorter, sharper and simpler? Apple's logo became simpler and sharper once they exchanged the rainbow colours for white.

My favourite short-sharp-simple object is the prehistoric hand-axe. It is self-explanatory.

Simplexity _{Ora Ïto}

> Good design is not about what you put in,
> it's about what you leave out.
> Peter Saville

> Simplicity shouldn't be simple, but complexity that has been tightened and synthesized. Nicolas Boileau.

> *Brevity, ornate conciseness, is the unique beauty of style.*
> Joseph Joubert

> Ideas well thought through enter the mind with ease.
> Joseph Joubert

> Stunningly obvious, with a surprise of incredible complexity.
> **Philippe Piguet commenting Georges Rousse's work.**

> **Everything simple is wrong; everything complicated is unusable.**
> Paul Valéry

Everything should be made as simple as possible, but not simpler. _{Einstein}

What is simple is not necessarily easy, but clearer.
What is simple is reduced to the essentials
and is self-sufficient. Sophie Péters

*Giotto and Matisse are very simple
and very complex at the same time.*
John Baldessari

Simplicity is the ultimate sophistication.

Léonardo da Vinci

I am tormented by the accursed ambition of always wanting to put a whole book in a page, a whole page in a sentence and that sentence in a word. That is who I am.
Joseph Joubert

KissKiss BankBank©.

TheThe exceptionexception thatthat provesproves thethe rulerule??

It is always impressive to see a master of elocution abridge and simplify. The artist sacrifices ornament for the line. All beautiful poems are simple
and coherent, without a single outstanding word;
a rarified expression would spoil them. Alain

LE MOT JUSTE...

...is a SHORT, SHARP AND SIMPLE French way of saying - in english - the appropriate, apt, applicable, convenient, correct, fitting, pertinent, opportune, proper, relevant, true, useful, adapted, becoming, befitting, belonging, right, well-suited, well-timed, just, concise and symbolic word.

THE RIGHT WORD?

The splendour of simplicity. Heidegger

Simple expression of complex thought. Donald Judd

Abridge…abridge ! Anton Chekhov

Weniger aber besser / *Less but better.* Dieter Rams

Simplicity is inexhaustible. Christian Bobin

Be human. Ernest Gowers. *Plain Words.*

I take everything away. *The essential remains.*
Raymond Savignac

25 words *or less.* Iggy Pop

Write less, *say more.* John Hegarty

Truth through simplicity. Sylvie Guillem. Ballerina.

Business should be simple. Michael O'Leary. Ryanair.

Plain Space. John Pawson

Laszlo Moholy-Nagy, then head of the Bauhaus school's foundation course, would ask students to make something from a single sheet of paper. They would inevitably create an array of elaborate pop-up panoramas and origami animals. Moholy-Nagy would look for a student who had simply folded the sheet and stood it up. Something that fully exploited the qualities of paper. This communicated the essence of the Bauhaus: where everything was stripped down to its most rational form through an intense study of materials, form and structure. An approach in which the abstract and the simple was always preferred to the figurative and the complex. **Edwin Heathcote**

Keep It Simple Stupid (KISS)

At HANDMADE™ everything was handmade. Short.

At HANDMADE™ everything was handmade. **Sharp.**

At HANDMADE™
everything was
handmade. **Simple.**

Bref: Long is often the road to short

31 PHOTOGRAPHY BRIEF

Nick Knight, arguably the most famous contemporary photographer, says he no longer is a photographer; but an image-maker. Judging by the popularity of filters on smartphone apps to manipulate photos into images, he may be right. But a strong culture in photography remains an essential – and curiously neglected - tool for branding that relies so much on images to create image. Multinationals outsource photographic responsibility to advertising agencies and photographers, often without giving their marketeers a grounding in the subject.

Nothing can replace shooting with world-class photographers to better understand how to obtain the desired outcome. Technique, although obviously necessary, is far from being why the best photographers are repeatedly chosen for important campaigns. An attitude, a point of view (literally), culture, empathy and an instinct for Zeitgeist are far more important.

A WONDERFUL PAINTING, BUT UPSIDE DOWN.

Photography is a magical thing. Under the black cloth, Dad lifts me up so that I can see the image he is going to take: a marvellous little painting full of colours, stunning and alive, but upside down. It's a small picture that is much prettier and clearer than the slice of reality we're looking at.

Jacques-Henri Lartigue. Diary. 1913.

*Everything begins from
the position of the camera.* Jeff Wall

In my experience, photography requires careful pre-planning but, more important still, a joyous management of the team's energy on D-day. The gladiator takes his decision in the arena.

The collection of quotations on the following pages reveals, I hope, how a desire for total control in photography is a grave mistake. Today, digital tools enable advertising agencies to show anxious clients finalised mock-ups that I would describe as dangerous " fake news ". This habit of wanting to reassure Marketing Directors and pre-sell to General Managers removes much of the chance for emotion to enter the final photo.

Just as the star-architects Jean Nouvel and Franck Gehry prefer an energetic drawing to express an idea, so should photographic campaigns spring from well-chosen words and inspirational doodles, rather than over-slick Photoshop inventions. Jean Nouvel speaks of a rough drawing as being " just an impulse " (élan) That is precisely my recommendation for an inspiring photo shoot brief.

If you look in your camera and see something you've seen before, don't click the shutter. Alexey Brodovitch

It is from the *subject itself* that I distill the image I want.
Irving Penn

Iconic : Use the camera's cyclopic vision

FIRST INSTINCTS

There is something special about one's natural, first instinct. In the days when large-format still life photography was taken on film, a whole day would be set aside for just one or two shots. 4x5 Colour Polaroids were used as trials before deciding to load the more expensive Ektachrome film. Seeing as one always imagines that things can be improved upon, the immediate reaction after looking at the first Polaroid, was to start fiddling with the set to improve the result. In time however, I adopted the thumb rule: " first Polaroid, first Ektachrome " , because I'd too often regretted the fresh spontaneity of the initial Polaroid that had been lost forever, unrecorded on proper film. If digital photography has now solved that problem of " lost " images, it has also somewhat unfortunately removed the " Polaroid pause ", when the photographer (and client) could physically hold the photo in his hands, analyse it and do trial croppings with two pieces of black L-shaped cardboard.

When I have found a landscape that I want to photograph, I wait for the right season, for suitable weather, and for the ideal time of day or night to capture the image that I know to be there.
Bill Brandt

**There are few things that
make me happier than discovering
a new way of seeing the familiar.**
Nick Knight

When I see something,
I don't take a photo of it.
*I think things look more beautiful
when they're not recorded.* Jeff Wall

I learnt later that Karl Lagerfeld considered the first
or second photo on a reel as often the best.
He also appreciated the fact that Helmut Newton would
shoot in five minutes, without an assistant.
This *"first is [often] best"* rule apparently applies to music
too. Tony Visconti, David Bowie's producer, reports
that the first take was almost always the finest.
Calligraphers who meditate before putting precious ink
and energy onto expensive vellum have probably
best mastered the art of creating the most favourable
conditions for immediate excellence.

*For a pseudo-scientific point of view on first instincts
and second thoughts, see the quotation by Tim Harford
on page 174.*

The subject speaks;
the lens looks.
[*L'object parle ; l'objectif voit.*]
Hugh Wilson.

studium / **punctum** → in a sense: **pleasure** / **ecstasy**.
Roland Barthes

HANDMADE
PHOTOGRAPHY BACKGROUND

I was determined to put all the lessons learnt at Lancôme into the photographic identity of HANDMADE™.
I was extremely fortunate in that Guido Mocafico, arguably the best still life photographer in the world today and with whom I had often shot for Lancôme, was kind enough to offer me two day's free shooting.

When I arrived at Guido's studio for the shoot, there was one nagging question I had still not managed to solve: the background colour. White would be too banal. Grey too Irving Penn. I had thought hard and long about it and still had no answer. As luck (serendipity ?!) would have it, Guido had just finished shooting a catalogue for Lobb shoes and said: " let's not waste time changing the set-up, you'll have to make do with this " creamy-stone-coloured 'Lobb' background " . To this day I still consider it the most beautiful background colour for a still life.

I'm not interested in a photo I can talk about before I take it.
Wolfgang Tillmans

HANDMADE
PHOTOGRAPHIC CONCEPT

I ended up by finding a distinct and simple photographic concept for Handmade: the police photography technique, or "mug shot". In other words, all the products were shot from both the top and the side, just as an architect systematically shows both the plan and elevation of a building. The camera was placed directly above the product, of which there were systematically two, so that one could be turned 90° on its side.

Simple as the "mug shot" approach may seem, it took me months and several shoots to see the initial trials gradually develop into a clear concept. This is just to say that what might look like an obvious idea often only fades slowly into view through patient observation and hard work.

HANDMADE
MAKING OF
A PHOTOGRAPH

I must have toyed with at least twenty ideas, over a three-week period before settling on the final direction.

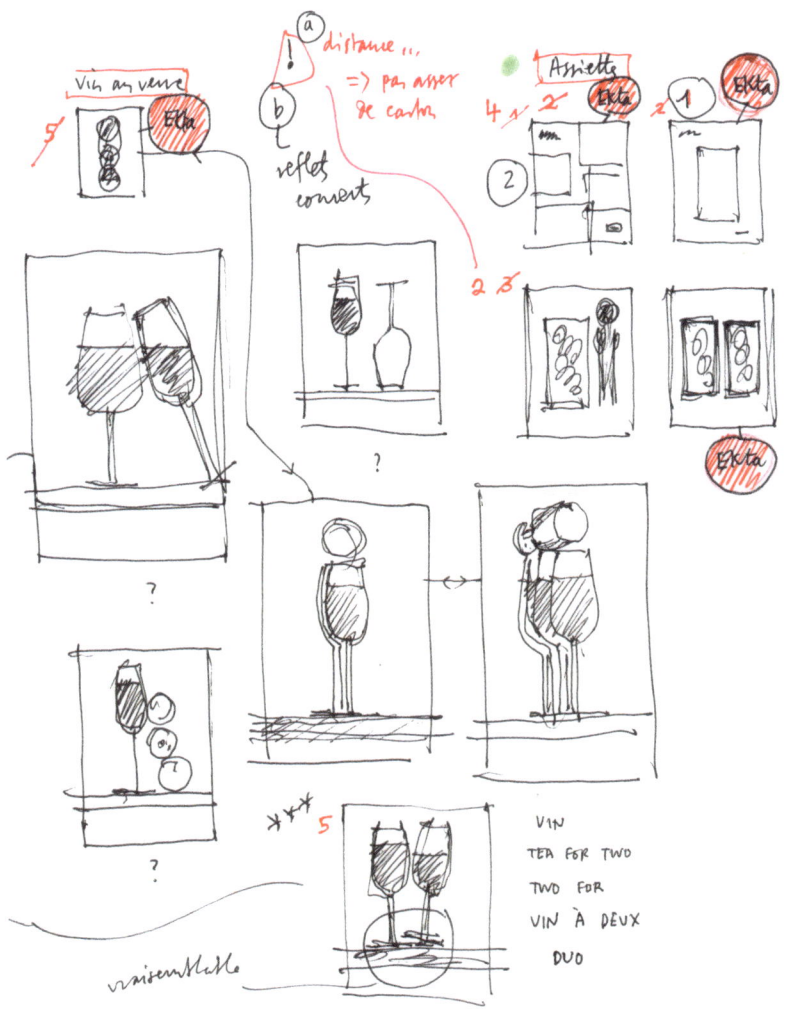

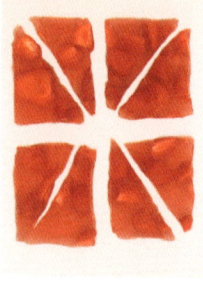

A BRAND IS AN ONION   31 - PHOTOGRAPHY BRIEF

32 WRITING ON THE BRAND WALL

> Branding is primarily about working with words and images. Both lead to ideas. That is no doubt why the chapters on photography and writing (which combine in the chapter on Picture-Thinking) are particularly dense. Brands need their own tone of voice, their idiosyncratic style of writing. To paraphrase Buffon's famous " Discourse to The French Academy ": *style is the brand.*

The following practical guidelines and rules of thumb on writing should however apply to all brands.

> Many authors admit that inspiration and desire often come from reading; poetry being especially stimulating. It is vital to create an animated and enthusiastic state of mind: nobody ever fumbles for their words when they are in a state of excitement. Listen to a taxi driver's eloquence when somebody dents his bumper. Such a mood will encourage writing with gusto and should kindle the ad-libbing genius of passionate conversation. Sleep on it; read it out aloud to your ears and modify if necessary. Finally, is the prose correct? The title itself of Robert Graves' handbook " The reader over your shoulder " sums it up.
> Write as if, poised like a parrot, your reader were inquisitively questioning the meaning of each word you write from over your shoulder. John Whale, in " Put it in Writing " gives similar advice: " keep your reader happy ". *Do as you would be done by.*

SIX RULES FOR WRITING
by George Orwell

A scrupulous writer, in every sentence that he writes, will ask himself at least four questions, thus:
- *What am I trying to say?*
- *What words will express it?*
- *What image or idiom will make it clearer?*
- *Is this image fresh enough to have an effect?*

And he will probably ask himself two more:
- *Could I put it more shortly?*
- *Have I said anything that is avoidably ugly?*

Speak straight. — Christian Bobin

Going from heart to heart. — Christian Bobin

Feign bile. — Jean Guitton

Photographic words. — Fernando Pessoa

Good prose is like a window pane. *George Orwell*

Writing is thinking in ink. — Alan Fletcher

Writing is thought itself. — Clément Rosset

Think in pictures. Write as you speak. Keep your reader happy.*

The pleasure of simple, precise, colourful words. Hugh Wilson [Clarins Editorial Guidelines]

Good writing *is bad writing well edited.* Kevin Ashton

* John Whale

WRITE *FAST* TALK

What can we writers learn from lizards, lift from birds? In quickness is truth. The faster you blurt, the more swiftly you write, the more honest you are. In hesitation is thought. In delay comes the effort for a style, instead of leaping upon truth which is the only style worth deadfalling or tiger-trapping. Ray Bradbury

---

We don't know what we wanted to say until we've said it.

Joseph Joubert

Most often it is when we press the keyboard of words that the idea appears.

It is as we speak, that we discover what we wanted to say.

Jean Guitton.

We should write like we write a letter, or as we talk. One word summons the next.

You should try to write as you would speak if you were talking at the top of your form, unhesitantly, in the idiom that best suited your theme and the occasion, and trusting your own ear. John Whale

SOUNDS LIKE SENSE

We are spontaneously more sensitive to sounds than to ideas. Paul Valéry

Take care of the sense, and the sounds will take care of themselves.

Lewis Carroll

The sense creates the sound. Joseph Joubert

WRITE *IN IMAGES*

Don't tell me the moon is shining; *show me the glint of light on broken glass.* Anton Chekhov

It's not to let people h we have to

Subtelty and nuances need to be coloured to be seen. Joseph Joubert

The poetic phrase or the metaphor is a universal meeting point. A way to find common humanity.

Valérie Dassonville.
Director of the Paris-Villette theatre.

I don't think in any language. I think in images.

Vladimir Nabokov

The poet's task is to show us a tree, before our brain tells us it's a tree.

Yves Bonnefoy. Poet.

fficient
r what we say;
ke it visible. ■ Joseph Joubert

Genuine poetry can communicate before it is understood.

For me, writing is above all about conjuring up images and communicating sensations.

Claude Simon

T.S. Eliot

In other words: Find your idiosyncratic tone of voice

HANDMADE
STORYTELLING

With HANDMADE™ I did my utmost to express
a "light-hearted but beautifully meaningful" tone
of voice on the rare items that contained words:
postcards and product labels. This shows that
the spirit of the brand can, and should,
be perceived wherever words are used.
I endeavoured to create an intriguing vibration
between the words and photos.

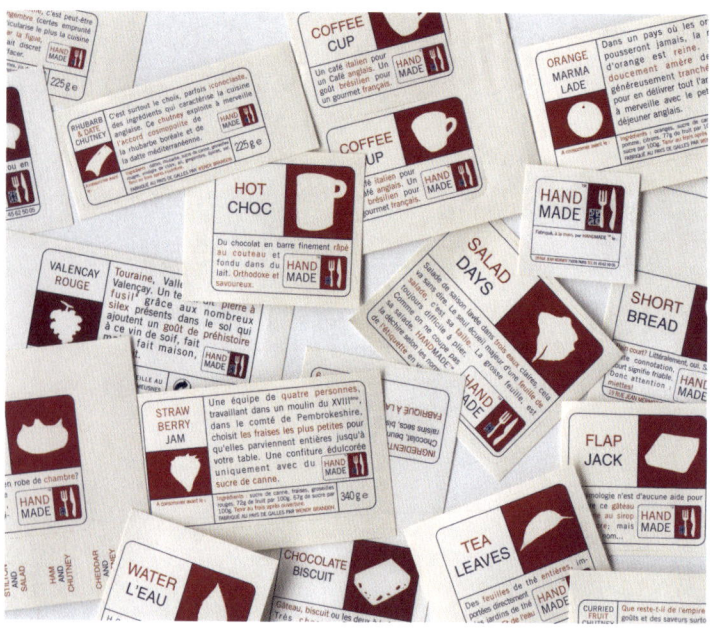

33 READING MATTERS

In an increasingly transparent and exhibitionistic world, people's reading habits and lists have become common knowledge. It is interesting that people in the heart of action and in positions of power give reading a prime, priority place in their daily routine. I admit that I didn't expect Barack Obama, when President, to have been capable of putting an hour aside a day to read and I was surprised to learn that Warren Buffet spends 80% of his time reading or thinking. Bill Gates, Elon Musk and Mark Zuckerberg all claim to be passionate readers.

> **The best books are those that tell you what you know already.**
> **George Orwell**

I have found that the economic theory of Marginal Utility (the additional satisfaction a consumer gains from consuming one more unit of a good or service) applies strongly to books and reading. You treasure most highly your newest book and are eager to read it, even before other volumes you still haven't finished. This has led me to make sure I read, annotate and digest books while they are still quite new, knowing that over time their satisfaction quotient will diminish sharply, like the value of a glass of water in the desert, once your thirst is quenched.

Beyond the pure pleasure factor, reading has to be the surest manner for people to increase their literacy, their way with words and therefore their brand's potential. Writers almost always « *warm up* » by reading, a habit that anyone can adopt. Flaubert would spend his mornings reading and his early afternoons daydreaming before ever putting quill to paper.

Some books are to be tasted,
others to be swallowed, and some
few to be chewed and digested:
that is, some books are to be read
only in parts; others to be read,
but not curiously; and some few
to be read wholly and with diligence
and attention. Francis Bacon. Philosopher.

*Where does the wind come from?
From an old book somone forgot to close.* Christian Bobin.

I am a passionate newspaper reader
every day, so many of my ideas come
from reading newspapers, or looking
in magazines or at TV, so that's the
reason why my images are connected
to what's going on in the world.
Andreas Gursky. Photographer

I am reading six books at once, the only way
of reading. Since, as you will agree, one book
is only a single unaccompanied note,
and to get the full sound, one needs ten others
at the same time. Virginia Woolf

*It is less important to read this or that book,
which is a waste of time, than to know
where it stands in relation to other books.*
Pierre Bayard. University Professor.

I never travel without books:
neither in peacetime, nor in wartime
(...) they are the best ammunition
I have found for this human journey.
Montaigne

To read is *to elect*.
Jean Guitton. Philosopher and theologian.

***Language is the limit* of our universe.**
Alberto Manguel. Author and Book historian.

We are what *we read*.
Martin Puchner. Philosopher.

Read again what you have read if you want to understand. Read again what you have read if you want to understand.

Joseph Joubert. Thinker. 1754-1824.

Books represent *a search for meaning* in a disordered and empty world.
Edwin Heathcote. Architect and journalist.

SO MANY BOOKS, *SO LITTLE TIME.*

Even a super reader (80 books a year) with a long life expectancy will finish a mere 5,000 books before they die. Those books shape you, as much as even friendships and the closest relationships do. They mark you strongly because the choice of what to read is so personal, the whispering voice of authors living or dead in your ear such a private set of relationships. For most readers, a lifetime reading plan must be steadily reworked to fall into line with your own passions and shifting interests. We are so busy, and a plan, however well-intentioned, can so easily become just another chore. It does make you think, though. How will you structure your reading life ? How might that become more rewarding or more startling ? What I recognise in my reading plan is hope and curiosity. It is not perfect. Nothing is. But over time, these plans bring in unexpected riches, and that is sufficient.

Nilanjana Roy. Author and journalist.

Why read? I'm asking you! Who learned anything from a book? There's only one good book, that's life.
Malcolm de Chazal. Mauritian poet, painter and writer.

TO PROGRESS OR TO PARACHUTE

Whereas a reader gradually makes his way through a book ; the internet user lands by parachute, without a map of the place. The reader has the advantage of a global vision, the internet user the advantage of the speed by which he reaches a scrap of fragmented knowledge through indexing links that never reveal their logic.

The transition from scroll to codex changed the way people read, notably freeing up one hand to take notes and add marginal comments.

How can you read a page without being able to fold its corner, or caress its grain, or hear it rustle when you turn it ?

Frédéric Potet. Journalist.

Mark my words Food for thought and action

I let oth
what I
say so

34 QUOTING QUOTATIONS

ers say,
ouldn't
vell.

Montaigne

The Ancient Greeks used quotations
as a figure of speech to establish
commonplace assertions [topoi].

I have adopted this practice, which explains why each
chapter of this book contains selected quotations
that illustrate the pros and sometimes cons of the subject.

It is not only how you say something that matters,
but also who said that something. Irving Penn has spent longer
thinking about photography than I have and George Orwell
devoted his life to " the joy of mere words " . I trust that
the following quotes on quotations will justify my method
whilst providing interest and enlightenment.

34 QUOTING QUOTATIONS

The intellectual extracts a sentence from its context to make it say *something else* that he considers either *more relevant* or *more in line with his own way of thinking* about things. Jean-François Bert

> An anthology of selected quotations can only hold its internal unity from the personality and tastes of the compiler himself, to whom it presents a kind of mirror.
> Simon Leys. Belgian-australian writer.

> There is nothing more original, nothing closer to oneself than to feed on others. But one has to digest them. The lion is made from assimilated sheep. Paul Valéry

A quotation is a door to a new idea.
Alan Fletcher

> I hate it when people say in approximate language and in poor style what an author has said so well.
> **Alain. Philosopher.**

> Maxims guide, direct and save indiscriminately. They are the thread in the labyrinth, the compass at night.
> **Joseph Joubert. Thinker.**

I have never scorned those from earlier generations, who spoke in quotations. It was undoubtedly better than what they themselves would have said. Alain. Philosopher.

I AM ACCUSED OF QUOTING WRITERS TOO MUCH.
But quotations are not screens behind which I take refuge. They are the formulation of a thought that one has once harboured and that one recognizes, beautifully expressed, by the pen of another. Quotations reveal the soul of the person who exhibits them. They betray the regret of not having known how to express one's own thoughts. **Sylvain Tesson. French writer & adventurer.**

Be personal, quote others.
Alan Fletcher

The bees plunder the flowers here and there, but afterward they make of them honey, which is all theirs; it is no longer thyme or marjoram. Even so with the pieces borrowed from others; he will transform and blend them to make a work that is all his own, to wit, his judgement. His education, work, and study aim only at forming this. **Montaigne**

Most people are other people. Their thoughts are someone else's opinions, their lives a mimicry, their passions a quotation. **Oscar Wilde**

One original thought is worth a thousand mindless quotings.
Diogenes Laërtius

Thought expressed in a sentence, whether grandiose or not, always presents itself as a world in itself, which tends to impose itself without discussion, without possible contradiction.
The charm and power of aphorisms lies in their peremptory aspect, which seems to reveal universal truths. *But there also lies their limit, even their danger. For a much more interesting thought arises from the permanent tension between several sentences, several points of view, several arguments that oppose and confront each other.* **Roger-Pol Droit. Philosopher.**

The modern genre of inspirational quotes is so bad that jokers have set up spoof-quote generators to run interference.
Janan Ganesh. Journalist.

i.e. If you couldn't have said it better

PUBLIC SPEAKING
SPEAKING WITH THE PUBLIC

Public speaking is about the public. What do they want to learn, how do they talk, what are they feeling? Your job is to transmit your emotions and feelings on a pertinent subject in the most genuine, enthusiastic and idiosyncratic manner possible. We are empathetic by nature. We are moved by what moves the speaker. Everybody has experienced tears welling to their eyes during a heartfelt speech at the funeral of a distant cousin twice-removed they have never even met.

1, 2, 3…

The secret of any art of expression is to say the same thing three times:
1 **you say you're going to say it,**
2 **you say it,**
3 **you say you said it.** Jean Guitton

"People don't remember what you say, but how you make them feel", said the poet Maya Angelou. I experienced this when teaching. Once, a foreign student who spoke little English and even less French stayed on at the last lesson of the year to thank me for the lectures. When I asked him why he had sat so assiduously in the front row, when I knew he couldn't have understood very much, he replied: " Oh! I came for your enthusiasm ". Everybody in the room wants to feel that you are talking to them, personally.

It's not what you say but how you say it.
Alan Fletcher

I use this sketch in a lesson on public speaking to illustrate how people should show their complete selves and align their speech and body language. In other words, remain as congruent and coherent with their Gesamtkunstwerk as possible.

To make a presentation is to become the captain of a cruise ship: *passengers must stay on board until disembarkation and find it interesting.*

Pia Martin

Breathing

is punctuation.

As one R.A.F. Squadron leader said: "After Churchill's speeches in June 1940, we wanted the Germans to come!"

By pausing,

you're taking time for people to get your message.

Paul-André Tavoillot

TO BE A GOOD AUCTIONEER…

…YOU NEED TO HAVE energy, charisma, confidence, patience, awareness, charm, and humanity.

…YOU NEED TO BE engaging, persuasive, entertaining, quick thinking, commanding, enthusiastic, passionate and fun. Hugh Edmeades. Christie's.

Every speech relies for its power on the common language of the tribe. It must, before anything else, connect its speaker to the audience. Sam Leith

The greatest leaders use a level of language equivalent to that of a college student. Adrien Rivierre

Public speaking is like a first date. It takes seven pieces of information contrary to the first impression to reverse a listener's initial opinion of a speaker. Anabelle Roberts

Understand and respect your audience. Involve them. Be enthusiastic and passionate. Tell a compelling story in words that are distinctly your own. You need to lead the listener along the road and spice up the trip with plenty of lions, tigers and bears. Monocle Magazine

The audience is the hero. Nancy Duarte

People come to see the races but also the exuberance and the energy you give off. Usain Bolt

Remember that on stage, you are both the piano and the pianist. The piano is your body that must not betray you (voice, posture, gestures and other signals that translate your body language). Then comes the work of the «pianist» who must interpret a melody to get the audience's support. Eléna Fourès

To do: Share your feelings with the listeners

36 ATTENTION IS A *CHISEL*.

Attention, concentration, and focus. To which you could add obsession and perseverance. These are the qualities that characterise artists and sporting heroes. But they are the universal tools for branding too. Artists and sportspeople are so absorbed in their passion that they find their way to a zone of effortless performance. Roger Federer and Glenn Gould come straight to mind. This is the power of paying attention.

Neuroscience is adamant: the brain cannot multitask. Overwhelmed with information, it tires itself out.
Caroline Cuny. Researcher.

Humans are able to perform two simple tasks at the same time, walking & talking for example. But the brain is not capable of performing multiple complex activities simultaneously. Sending a text message in a meeting takes 50% longer, and the risk of error is 50% greater.
Caroline Talbot

You can't be split three different ways on your laptop, phone or having a conversation – as we always are. Crafting requires a steady mind.
Yelena Ford.
Managing Director of *The New Craftsmen*.

Our attention cannot focus on a single topic for more than ten minutes. The reason for this is biological: in a sustained mode of activity, the brain emits waves at a very high frequency, of the order of 40 Hertz, which sucks up a vast amount of the body's total energy.
Pierre-Marie Lledo.
Director of neurosciences at l'Institut Pasteur.

Internet, social media and pocket screen applications in general do their best, or worst, to take your attention away from you. Interruptions through notifications are especially dangerous. Scientific studies say it takes 20 minutes to get back to where you left off. The author Yuval Noah Harari says he doesn't own a smartphone for fear of distraction. And university professor Matthew B. Crawford spends half his week mending motorbikes to force himself to remain in real life (IRL).

Keep your eye on the ball !
Hugh Wilson

Attention is the chisel of memory.
**Pierre-Marc Gaston.
Second Duc de Lévis. [1764-1830]**

Troops must be either at "attention!" or "at ease!" Neither half-work nor half-rest is to be tolerated. Jean Guitton

10 INFORMATIONS *MAXIMUM*

The brain makes an initial selection of all information, but beyond ten elements, our mind can no longer categorise and will just process information automatically. The whole of the working memory - the one dedicated to immediacy - becomes saturated. Now in our digital environments, this limit of ten elements is very quickly reached. Gaëtan de Lavilleon. Professor of Neuroscience.

Cave canem : Pay attention or you'll pay for it

LEARNING & TEACHING

A BRAND IS A SCHOOL

In the 1990s, L'Oréal definitely was THE marketing school in France. Each ex-graduate-brand-manager was given self-taught schooling by being encouraged to work with the best creative talents and learn from them. Giving marketeers the time to train with fragrance bottle designers, perfumers, photographers and semiologists, not to mention their peers, is the most important investment a brand can make.
I very much like a remark made by Christian Blanckaert, who used to work for Hermès and is now President of the J.M. Weston foundation: " there are no books on know-how, so it's all about transmission ".

We can only ever tell the story of our own lives and the universe around ourselves. Alain

What do you do for a living?
Nothing, I'm learning.
Learning what?
Nothing, I'm learning.
Christian Bobin

The value of a person's intelligence lies not so much in its science (dictionaries are at hand) as in the possession of active habits which enable him to adapt his knowledge and principles to the singularity of ever new cases, and conversely to discern what nourishment he can derive from what is offered to him by chance. Jean Guitton

Education is the most powerful weapon which you can use to change the world. Nelson Mandela

He who dies without transmitting dies a thief.
Michel Germond

> Seeds are what should be sprinkled into people's minds, not dead trees and all manner of plants. Joseph Joubert

LEARNING & REVERSE-TEACHING

I discovered the wisdom of crowds in my first year of teaching marketing. After a few lessons I was obliged to urgently provide the students with a mid-term mark. Somewhat caught out by surprise, I simply asked the class to spend an hour writing down what they had learnt so far.
I quickly noticed that if I took one or two quotations from each of the sixty students' copies, the compilation was more original, interesting and amusing than my own lectures.

My faith and confidence in the younger generations has been systematically confirmed, over the years, through numerous examples. Be it a common sense attitude to the downside of the digital world, or a desire to share their knowledge with the class. The takeaway is simple: the more you give, the more you get given back. You learn reverse-teaching, which is learning from teaching. It is exactly the same principle as mentoring and reverse-mentoring.
To coin Blanckaert's phrase above, there are no books on savoir-vivre, so it's all about transmission.

> Curiosity is an impulse just like hunger and thirst : accumulating information about our environment is also a means of survival.
>
> **Stanislas Dehaene. Neuroscientist.**

> Original thinkers are life-long learners.
> Simon Kuper

> Curiosity is the very salt of life.
> Renaud Capuçon

> I'm driven by a need to increase my own understandings.
> David McCandless

> I like to open the doors to people's brains.
> Philippe Starck

> To innovate is first of all to train well.
> Xavier Fontanet

> The mind is not a vessel to be filled, but a fire to be kindled.
> Plutarch

> You teach less what you know than what you are.
> Jean Jaurès

> When the robots awaken, the only solution will be education. *Don't teach anything, because you still have everything to learn.*
> Pessoa

> If I don't learn anything new, I'm dead.
> Clint Eastwood

Always go from the known
to the unknown.

Jean Guitton

Graduating experience
is the art of instruction.

Alain

**I cannot teach
anybody anything.
I can only
make them think.**

Socrates

The digital revolution will soon
make diplomas obsolete.

Olivier Babeau (2019)

Since I didn't study anything, I learned a lot.

Anatole France

Diploma. Sign of science.
Doesn't prove anything.

Gustave Flaubert (1911)

I don't teach, I tell.

Montaigne

I teach myself.

Hugh Wilson

Result : The reciprocal joy of transmission

38 BEAUTY SAVES

> The French writer and adventurer Sylvain Tesson
> disagrees with Dostoevsky's famous remark:
> "beauty will save the world",
> affirming that "beauty can save mankind".
> Surely therefore beauty can save brands.

Perhaps unsurprisingly for a country obsessed with the good things in life, the French have two nouns for beauty, to only one in english: "la beauté" (beauty) and "le beau" (that which is beautiful). The French thinker Joseph Joubert gives an interesting explanation of the nuance between the two: "la beauté touche les sens et le beau touche l'âme" [la beauté touches the senses and le beau touches the spirit].

Nothing is more beautiful than emptiness. **Coco Chanel**

Beauty will save the world and art is its instrument.
Vladimir Soloviev

This perhaps points to the difference between the decorative arts, that seem to best portray beauty when the usefulness of things is evident, and the fine arts [Beaux-Arts in French!] that provoke emotions. Both the French philosopher Alain and the English art critic Ruskin agree that beauty in an object is linked to its visible use. A point of view shared by the contemporary Italian artist Giuseppe Penone, famous for his tree sculptures.

> It's not sufficient for something to be beautiful, it must be appropriate to the subject. **Blaise Pascal**

In order to doubt, one must first be sure; therefore beauty must come before truth.

Alain. Philosopher.

For brands to try and create beauty on a regular basis, my view is that one should aim for (though obviously not necessarily attain) Edmund Burke's sublime, rather than just beauty. Roland Barthes, when talking of the quality of a photograph that moves you, talks of feeling ecstasy rather than of just feeling pleasure.

A truly beautiful object resembles its idea. Joseph Joubert

**To find beauty, you have to think of anything but.
Art is the flower of what is useful.** Alain. Philosopher.

To conclude this sideline into French vocabulary and culture, in agreement with Joseph Joubert, my view is that brands should pursue *" le beau"*, not just *" la beauté "*.

Beauty is the child of the coherent relationship between parts.
Alan de Botton. Philosopher.

Deep beauty is also goodness. In Greek, kallos expresses both.

Renzo Piano

IMPERFECT BEAUTY

There is no beauty without some strangeness in the proportions.
Christopher Marlowe

True beauty is never solemn.
True beauty always has a certain nonchalance to it.
Christian Bobin

Strangeness is the indispensable condiment of all beauty.
Charles Baudelaire

Beauty needs no explanation.
It cannot be questioned.
It has divine right of sovereignty.
Oscar Wilde

WABI-SABI:
A beauty of things imperfect, impermanent and incomplete.
Emma Peascod. Artist.

Temples always have an odd number
of gaps and an even number of columns,
in order to direct the axial gaze towards a void
and not a meagre feature. **René Pechère**

Beauty summons us to think.

Alain. Philosopher.

All beauty is idiosyncratic.

François Cheng. Author.

Beauty is born from what is useful.

Alain. Philosopher.

We refuse perfection.

Philippe Saglio. Art Director.

Beauty is truth, truth beauty.

John Keats. Poet.

The beauty of what is.

Yves Bonnefoy. Poet.

Golden thread. Beauty is probably the golden thread to branding

39 TRUTH *IS BEAUTY*

THE PLAIN TRUTH. THE BEAUTY OF THE BANAL.
The truth is often more astounding than fiction.
Documentaries and sport prove this on a regular basis.
It is also this belief that led to the German photographic tradition of Neue Sachlichkeit (*new objectivity*) in the 1920s, followed by the Düsseldorf School, influenced by Bernd and Hilla Becher, in the 1970s. The impressionist painter Cézanne wanted his hand to take the feelings and sensations straight from the scene to his canvas, without any influence from his mind or reason.
The impossible truth.

I agree with the photographer Tim Walker who considers photography should be a real moment. The Financial Times weekend supplement once did a fashion shoot underwater with enormous sharks swimming around near the model. It could no doubt have been faked using Photoshop, but as the *"making of"* showed, truth is more telling than trickery. My conviction is that brand photography should be, if not altogether true, at least likely, probable, straightforward, plausible, believable, credible, realistic, feasible and conceivable. *"Vraisemblable"* in French.

MAGNA EST VERITAS ET PRAEVALET

[Great is truth and it prevails]
The Bible

Great graphic design is about truth:
a *perfect reduction of thought into a line.*
Harry Pearce. Pentagram.

I've always been of the view that
if you can do it for real, then do it for real.
It looks real, because it is real.
Gary Powell. James Bond film stunt co-ordinator.

Beauty is truth, *truth beauty.* John Keats

Truth is more precious than beauty. André Comte-Sponville. Philosopher.

For fashion photography to resonate, for people to believe in it, *it has to be a real moment.* Tim Walker. Photographer.

**Actually, I'm interested in the truth.
I'm not here to manipulate people.
Quite the contrary.
I don't put a filter on life.
It's about not blinking.**

Steve McQueen. Artist.

Verily Sincerity can be felt

OBSESSION

OBSESSIONS ARE PASSIONS

To be obsessive about something is generally perceived as negative. I have never consciously collected quotations on obsessions, but one long week-end
I happened to go to five art exhibitions in three days: Picasso, Giacometti, Basquiat, Schiele and Nadar. The overpowering impression I came away with was just how much energy, work and obsession they all gave their art.

That led me to create a link between the words artistic and autistic*. Only a letter apart. When I showed the two words on a slideshow to my graphic art students, they seemed to agree, as many of them whipped out their smartphones to photograph the silver screen. Later, the search bar in my database quickly revealed quotations that prove there is a strong connection between having an obsession and producing interesting work. When going through my notebooks in preparation for this book, I quickly realised that quotations and large-format cameras were probably my obsessions, as you can see from my doodles on page 252/253. I now therefore believe that to be obsessive is positive.

*Recently a student informed me that Jean-Louis Aubert, lead singer of the French group Telephone, had produced a song called: "Artiste, Autiste". Minds think alike. Great or not.

ARTISTIC

I hope people will understand my obsession with buildings and objects, with creating meaning and sensitivity. Jean Nouvel

Steve Jobs reminds us, not without a touch of malice, that the only obsession of a leader should be to create exciting products and an inspiring world. As for profit, that will be come as a bonus!
Armand Hatchuel. Professor.

You can't do things if obsessiv

Because I'm never content. Because I like the idea of obsessive meticulousness. Because the first shot must always be corrected. I always rewrite, correct and annotate my books.

Sylvain Tesson. Author.

The first preparatory phase consists of taking ownership of an issue with obsession. The aim is to create mental images of the problem so that you can take them with you everywhere.

Alain Connes, 72. Mathematician.
Fields Medal 1982.

All of Eileen Gray's furniture showed her personal touch of humour and irony. One can sense a need for playfulness, bordering on obsession, in the elements that fold, turn and snap into place.

Peter Adam. Film maker.

Be crazy, be obsessed, trust your obsession and work crazy!

Student at Penninghen

exceptional ou're not yourself.

Nicolas Bouzou. Economist.

Family albums are very boring. I'm only interested in images that show a fascination, an obsession.

Erik Kessels. Collector.

A fight as solitary as it is obsessive, like the pointless quest of a madman in his padded cell.

Philip Roth. *Why Write?*

With each book, Haruki Marakami finds a new metaphor to illustrate his obsession.

Florence Noiville

A filing cabinet exposes a person's obsessions.

Jean-François Bert

Perhaps : Depth is a quality

# OBSESSION

My delight in large-format cameras dates back to my first advertising shots as a Brand Manager.

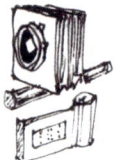

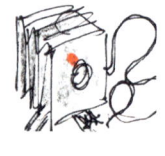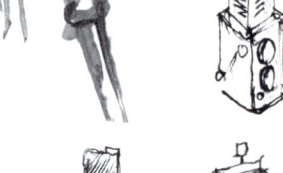

The objects themselves are such a beauty to behold that I ended up buying my own.

41 GESAMTKUNSTWERK
[TOTAL WORK OF ART]

All young children are encouraged to be polymaths, to be all-rounders. Stone-age men and women must have been "jacks-of-all-trades". They had to be. But our education systems and business environment seem to have been worried that we would all become "masters of none" and have therefore specialised us, with practical, one-trade labels. This reduces people to what they have done before, rather than what they might become in the future.

The rare people who sometimes manage to escape from the labelling system are certain artists and designers. Only the world-renowned ones, mind you. If you are under the radar, then you are pigeon-holed as a calligrapher, a water-colour painter or a sculptor. But certain Art Directors such as Tom Ford, Karl Lagerfeld, Hedi Slimane and Virgil Abloh succeed in escaping nomenclature. They become what Wagner described as a "Gesamtkunstwerk". Or, as Goethe said of himself: "*a collective singular consisting of several persons with the same name*".

Being marketed doesn't suit me.
Pigeonholing is for pigeons.
Jessye Norman

I live my life as an artwork.
Daniel Lismore

I want to be
everything I am.
Chimamanda Ngozie Adiche

I am a multi-indisciplinary artist.
Serge Mansau

ALL I DO

I highly advocate the freedom for all to express the wide variety of different traits of character that form each person's singularity and enable us all to become Gesamtkunstwerke. Entrepreneurs and brand creators are, almost by definition, obliged to be one-man-bands. I am no trained photographer or graphic artist, but found it indispensable - for HANDMADE - to use my amateur talents in those fields to avoid having to depend upon buying in outsourced artwork.

Be yourself. Everyone else is already taken.
Oscar Wilde

Reproducing the world around me using the world inside me.
Goethe

Brands are rarely encouraged to extend their elasticity beyond their initial domain of specialisation, their core business. But the stronger the brand character, the wider the possible scope. Hermès, Armani, Bulgari and Chanel have all branched out into areas such as hotels, home furnishings, bicycles etc. There is however a limit to what consumers accept. Chanel put their logo on a surfboard to the immediate mockery of social media. And a famous pâtisserie brand in Paris, well known for their macaroons, thought it could – fairly logically I thought - branch out into sandwiches, but the consumers wouldn't follow. They obliged the brand to stay put, in its original space of skill.

ALL I AM.

In a nutshell A Brand is a sphere of shared emotions

42 IDIOSYNCRASY AND GENIUS

The word idiosyncratic is little used by the French. However the French author André Gide gives an excellent definition, when he says: " idiosyncrasy is our disease of values ". As if our true selves were engrained (*literally dyed*) into our fibres, sinews and cells. You therefore have to live with your idiosyncrasies, just as you would with an incurable disease. Idiosyncrasy has the same Greek stem idio- [cf idiom and idiot] which means personal, private, peculiar, separate or distinct. These are words that apply to branding. Every brand should be particular and singular. Perhaps the over-used scientific term DNA should be replaced by brand idiosyncrasy.

We have to make do with who we are. Marie-Astrid d'Andigné. Penninghen Student.

Or perhaps brand genius? The Romans gave every person a tutelary god or attendant spirit to preside over their destiny throughout life. Brand building could be considered in the same manner. Genius and idiosyncrasy should be engrained in every brand at birth.
Once inside, it should last for ever.

There's no escaping your way of doing things.
Jean Echenoz. Author.

We are all worms. But I do believe that I am a glow worm.
Winston Churchill

The crazier, the better. Hugh Wilson

Embrace your raw strange magic.
Casey Gerald

There was never a genius *without a tincture of madness.*
Aristotle

You can treat neurosis, *but you can't cure yourself.* Sartre

Genius is born crazy. Moncler

I don't want to be normal. Karl Lagerfeld

A genius is the one most like himself. Thelonious Monk

The peculiar genius.
T Magazine on Björn Borg

Always on the fringe. Apart. Irrevocably singular and as such, alone.
Philippe-Jean Catinchi on Topor

Making your unknown known is the important thing.
Georgia O'Keefe

El Greco, "mad genius".
Théophile Gautier

I'm not special, *I'm unique.* Kevin Systrom

It takes a long time to sound like yourself.
Miles Davis

Stick to your share of irregularity,
make the impossibility of allowing yourself to be described or of falling into line a value of life and creation;
in the gentlest possible way.
Roland Barthes.

Synopsis: Perhaps the key to branding is ingrained singularity

43 THE DIFFICULT BALANCE

The Medieval theologian Saint Thomas Aquinas would systematically insert the phrase " *sed contra est* " [but the opposite exists / on the contrary] into his writings. Indeed there are always two sides to every coin.
Montaigne even had a coin engraved with a pair of scales as a metaphor to accompany his motto " *what do I know?* ".

If delight and amazement are often to be enjoyed towards the more extreme scale of actions, a certain degree of balance is still required to avoid a fatal pitfall as every cyclist knows when negotiating corners on riding downhill. Both Confucius and Nietzsche exhort us to aim for the " appropriate balance ". What is deemed appropriate is subjective, but I suppose rock 'n roll, the mini skirt or the E-type Jaguar could all be seen more as " the difficult balance " rather than "the middle ground ".

These Scandinavian designs perfectly encompass the concept of "lagom", which means "neither too little nor too much". The Financial Times

Since both extremes are harmful, the middle path must be adopted and that is not easy to determine.
Robert Burton. 1577-1640.

The test of a first-rate intelligence is the ability to hold two opposed ideas in mind at the same time and still retain the ability to function. F. Scott Fitzgerald

OXYMORON : A rhetorical figure by which contradictory terms are conjoined so as to give point to the statement or expression. The Oxford English Dictionary

It's the balance, the difficult balance, that interests me in a man. Alain

THE FEDERER QUOTIENT

There is such a thing as the optimal amount of devil in a person, and *it is not zero*. Call it the Federer Quotient.
Federer has a controlled dose of the dark stuff. Janan Ganesh

Opposites are as one. The most beautiful of harmonies are born out of dissonance. Everything is born from oppositions. Heraclitus.

The delicate balance must endlessly be renegotiated. It is never perfect. Sarah Bakewell

You always have to push back the limits, without being foolhardy. Stand on the edge, at the limit of equilibrium.
Virgilio Martinez. Peruvian chef.

There are only two things worthwhile in art;
        1° The flash of authority.
        2° The flash of hesitation.
        That is all.
One is made of the other, but at the summit
the two are very clearly distinguishable.
        Nicolas de Staël

At Chanel, we attach as much importance to natural raw materials as we do to synthetic molecules. Chanel N°5 depends as much on the quality of the jasmine as on the aldehydes. It's the balance that counts. Christopher Sheldrake. Perfumer.

In all that is beautiful, I feel the **struggle between inspiration and rules**; *everything is contained and restrained*; the bonds are stretched under the strain but do not break; it is like *Prometheus in chains.*

Alain. Philosopher.

Think like a strategist, **act like a primitive.**
René Char

It's all a *question of measure.*
Christian Bobin

I like the rule that corrects emotion,
I like the emotion that corrects the rule.
Georges Braque

I seek **the eternal** and **the ephemeral**
at the same time.
Georges Perec

We must work with both *freedom*
and rectitude.
Fabienne Verdier

Not too hot and *not too cold.* **Just right.**
Goldilocks

Act as a man of thought
and think as a man of action.
Henri Bergson

Give me the temperance
to keep a middle ground.
Saint Thomas Aquinas

I'm here to break the rules
but *keep the traditions.*
Alexander McQueen

We organize a dialectic between
the planned and *the random.*
Rem Koolhaas

Living for today and tomorrow
at the same time.
Tal Ben-Shahar

I am *neither one* nor *the other.*
Marguerite Duras

Beyond the appearance of self-confidence,
the leader cultivates doubt.
Les Echos

**Truth is the balance point
between two contradictions.**
Chinese Proverb

Conclusion: Equilibrium is a never-ending quest

MY TAKE ON EACH CHAPTER

1. *Id Est:* Everything a brand does is branding
2. *Perchance* Alert minds gather string
3. *When?* Kairos is a powerful lever to success
4. *Autrement dit:* Don't underestimate the power of colour
5. *In a word:* Manners maketh brands
6. *Pour info:* Names shape behaviour
7. *Verdict:* Vitality is a virtue
8. *B.C./A.D.* All is not digital. Stand on the bridge
9. *Fundamental:* Culture gives and makes sense
10. *P.S.* The future is built on the past
11. *Proven:* Emotions trump thoughts
12. *In short:* Small changes make a big difference
13. *Believe me!* Startuppers become Davids versus
14. *Ready?* Prepare and anticipate
15. *Reality:* Uncertainty and unfairness are the norm
16. *Mix:* Balance order and disorder
17. *Counsel.* Work hard playfully
18. *Daily:* Be regular, open and persistent
19. *Nota Bene* Simple, humble rules and behaviour
20. *FYI* Gather knowledge for future action
21. *N.B.* Create an efficient and personal encyclopedia

22 I.D. Stimulating ideas energize
23 Eureka: Practice using your subconscious
24 C-à-d: Giving carte blanche generates a black hole
25 To sum up: Net sales follow creative actions
26 P.P.S. Mastering a certain degree of technique is essential
27 Videlicet Look hard, often and again
28 Kurz gesagt Fragments are easy to share and to remember
29 Viz. Make ideas visible
30 Bref: Long is often the road to short
31 Iconic: Use the camera's cyclopic vision
32 In other words: Find your idiosyncratic tone of voice
33 Mark my words Food for thought and action
34 i.e. If you couldn't have said it better
35 To do: Share your feelings with the listeners
36 Cave canem: Pay attention or you'll pay for it
37 Result: The reciprocal joy of transmission
38 Golden thread Beauty is probably the golden thread to branding
39 Verily Sincerity can be felt
40 Perhaps: Depth is a quality
41 In a nutshell A Brand is a sphere of shared emotions
42 Synopsis: Perhaps the key to branding is ingrained singularity
43 Conclusion: Equilibrium is a never-ending quest

ONION TYPE DESIGN - OTD

In a book on branding, the very least we could do was create a specific typeface. After all, the word character that designates a graphic symbol is also the distinctive trait one looks for in a brand.

Axel Vagnard created OTD [Onion Type Design] at the very beginning of this project. Our desire was for the typeface to be both simple and easy to read when in small print and yet bold and striking when used in large format.

This double quality is due to the ink traps that prevent the coloured pigment from bleeding, thus ensuring crisp edges in small print and graphic vigour when enlarged.

```
ABCDEFGH      0123    abcdefgh
IJKLMNOP      4567    ijklmnop
QRSTUVWXYZ    8&9     qrstuvwxyz


ABCDEFGH      0123    abcdefgh
IJKLMNOP      4567    ijklmnop
QRSTUVWXYZ    8&9     qrstuvwxyz
```

Available for purchase @studioaxelvagnard

Beautifully nostalgic ligatures join certain letters, forming patterns that shape

æ œ ct st fi ffi ffi ty

style

one hundred and sixty 7° Italic

five

glyphs

A font based on ROMAN CALLIGRAPHY

with cracks to let the light in...

ink on paper æsthetics

NEXT STEPS

Time stands still for no man, or woman, or book.

I can therefore only hope that the ideas contained in this short manual are sufficiently vibrant to help the reader over the long term and that the contents are sufficiently rich to merit a re-read.

You can also continue to discover my findings and thoughts on my Instagram account @hughwilsonparis

Thank you for your reading this far.

I told you I couldn't teach you anything; but perhaps you might have learnt something.

ICONOGRAPHY CREDITS

Christopher Wilson took the 4 " x 5 " portrait of the author p. 6.

My thanks to **Gilles Laurent** for his technical and moral help for the large format scans pp. 17, 28-29, 70-71, 100-101, 138-139, 146-147, 201, 220.

Guido Mocafico shot the 14 HANDMADE posters and views of the restaurant in his idiomatic 8 " x 10 " Sinar-style pp 28-29, 88-89, 94-95, 179.

Claire Boit and Florence Verrier were indispensable in helping me shoot all the other large format HANDMADE photographs, the black light bulb and the walnut pp 47, 141, 159, 161, 190-191, 202-203, 209, 210, 212-213, 221.

Salomé Lelièvre took the tongue-in-cheeek photos of François, Christopher and John p. 53.

Jacques Dirand took the sunny photograph of the HANDMADE restaurant p. 82-83.

The photograph of the kayak p. 104-105 was most probably taken by **the Marlborough College Sports teacher.**

Adrien Dewisme created the cyanotype onions p. 268.

THANKS

Every author owes much to many: from inspirational schoolteachers to work colleagues, friends and family. Perhaps the simplest way to express my sincerest thanks is to list those who, in alphabetical order, have over the years - and perhaps unbeknown to them - been significant in enabling me to accumulate the knowledge, experience and know-how to produce this book.

All my students at Penninghen, José-Manuel Albesa, Daniel Aubin, Babou, Julia Bennett, Véronique Berthon, Maurice Biriotti, Claire Boit, Whitney Bolin, Céline Bréger, Robin Child, Edouard Corbière, Philippe Dapsanse, Ghislain de Villoutreys, Helen Denno, Joseph Dirand, André Dubreuil, Mr Eastwood, François-Xavier Germain, Joanna Gilfeather, Noëlle Herpeux, Laurent Houel, René Jodelet, Dimitri Katsachnias, Valentin Lautier, Guido Mocafico, Edgard Montjean, Meryl Perradin, Philippe Phan, Jean-Luc Pouthier, Charles Ramuz, Etienne Robial, Alain Roulot, Colette Roussaux, Marc Saunder, Philip Shearer, Vincent Thilloy, Axel Vagnard, Florence Verrier, Maurizio Volpi, Johanna Worth, John D Wilkinson.

Special thanks to **Margaret E. Goss**
           & **Major Ian H.G. Wilson**
whose enthusiastic belief in education is still alive.

BOOK DESIGN BY AXEL VAGNARD

A book, above all else, is a self-portrait. The genius of Axel Vagnard's design for A Brand is an Onion is that people who know me say: "the book is you!" One cheeky French friend even said he could hear my accent.

Axel started by designing the typeface " OTD " : Onion Type Design that you are reading here (see page 266-267 for details), before choosing the definitive title – from the 285 different choices I had been toying with. He then patiently crafted the layout that has a clear, idiosyncratic style, without any two pages ever looking the same, giving form to my thoughts. **A sculpture of friendship, for which I am most profoundly grateful.**

MY THANKS TO LES ÉDITIONS ODYSSÉE

Alain Escourbiac is the master printer who very kindly helped produce a self-funded beta version of this book. He is also the owner of Les Editions Odyssée, specialized in the exquisite crafting of books on photography and more.

The young editor (and photographer), Yegan Mazandarani, is as curious and interested in as many subjects as myself. His quiet, unassuming, and precious advice has been vital in transforming the first draft into this beautiful new book.

I feel very lucky that A Brand is an Onion should have benefited from the encouragement and help of such a team.
An example of alignment at work.

ÉDITIONS ODYSSÉE

Texts
Hugh Wilson

Artistic Direction
Axel Vagnard

Graphic and Typographic Design
Axel Vagnard

Production
Escourbiac l'Imprimeur, Graulhet

English proofreading
Julia Bennett, Helen Denno and Joanna Gilfeather

Editorial Direction
Yegan Mazandarani

Typefaces used
Akzidenz Grotesk Bold by The Berthold Foundry 1896
Onion Type Design by Axel Vagnard 2019

Paper
Arena White Rough 120g

INDEX

Acknowledgements : The author would like to extend his thanks to the following publications for providing quotes as indicated herein:

PRESS.
Harvard Business Review, Intelligent Life, Les Echos, Le Figaro, Le Monde, Monocle, The Economist, The Financial Times, The New York Times, The Guardian.

Abrahamson, Eric. Management professor. 117
Adam, Peter. (1929-2019) British film maker. 251
Adichie, Chimamanda Ngozie. Nigerian writer. 254
Agnew, Harriet. English journalist. 55, 118
Alain. (1868-1951) aka Emile Chartier. French philosopher. 7, 32, 37, 49, 86, 87, 145, 151, 154, 158, 160, 161, 175, 180, 182, 199, 228, 236, 239, 242, 243, 245, 259, 261
Albert, Eric. French Management consultant. 133
Alikavavazovic, Jakuta. French author. 61
Amabile, Teresa M. Professor of Business Administration. 131
Angelou, Maya. (1928-2014) American poet. 230
Apollinaire, Guillaume. (1880-1918) French poet. 79
Aquinas, Saint Thomas. (1225-1274) Medieval Italian theologian and philosopher. 258, 263
Arad, Ron. Israeli industrial designer. 148
Aristotle. (384 B.C. - 322 B.C.) Greek Philosopher. 73, 140, 173, 257
Arnault, Bernard. French businessman. 45, 55, 96, 109
Ashfaq, Mohammed Qasim. British Artist. 78
Ashton, Kevin. British technology pioneer. 120, 122, 166, 215
Atkins, James. Chairman at Vertis Environmental Finance. 133
Aubert, Jean-Louis. French singer and songwriter. 248
Aulet, Bill. Managing Director of The Martin Trust Center for MIT entrepreneurship. 93
Babeau, Olivier. French Professor and economist. 66, 239
Bacon, Francis. (1561-1626) English philosopher. 65, 223
Bacon, Francis. (1909-1992) Irish-born, British painter. 99, 192
Bakewell, Sarah. British author and professor. 260
Baldessari, John. (1931-2020) American conceptual artist. 199
Balenciaga, Cristobal. (1895-1972) Spanish fashion designer. 149
Barber, Jerry. Golfer. 37
Barbotte, Didier. French blacksmith. 117
Baricco, Alessandro. Italian writer, director and performer. 26
Barthes, Roland. (1915-1980) French semiotician and professor. 111, 112, 188, 207, 243, 257
Baselitz, Georg. German painter. 149
Basquiat, Jean-Michel. (1960-1988) American Artist. 147
Baudelaire, Charles. (1821-1867) French poet. 113, 121, 244
Bayard, Pierre. French professor of literature. 73, 186, 223

Beckett, Samuel. (1906-1989) Irish playwright. 166, 171
Ben-Shahar, Tal. American and Israeli teacher of positive psychology. 263
Benjamin, Walter. (1892-1940) German philosopher. 116
Bergé, Pierre. French businessman. 73
Berger, John. (1926-2017) English Art critic. 143
Bergson, Henri. (1859-1941) French philosopher. 65, 73, 262
Bert, Jean-François. French sociologist. 142, 143, 228, 251
Berthoz, Alain. French neurophysiologist. 74
Bertin, Rose. (1747-1813) French milliner. 86
Beyer, Frédérick Mispelblom. Professor of Sociology. 133
Bezos, Jeff. American businessman. 26, 92
Bible, The. 6, 147, 148, 246
Bickford-Smith, Coralie. Penguin book cover designer. 175
Blanckaert, Christian. French businessman. 236, 237
Bobin, Christian. French author and poet. 27, 49, 145, 149, 155, 160, 167, 168, 200, 215, 223, 236, 244, 262
Boileau, Nicolas. (1636-1711) French poet. 151, 198
Bolt, Usain. Jamaican sprinter. 233
Bompard, Alexandre. French businessman. 93
Bonnefoy, Yves. (1923-2016) French poet. 219, 245
Borg, Björn. Swedish tennis player. 257
Bosc, Emmanuelle. French journalist. 73
Bossuet. (1627-1704) French theologian, orator and stylist. 125
Bouzou, Nicolas. French economist. 251
Bradbury, Ray. (1920-2012) American author. 152, 216
Brandt, Bill. (1904-1983) German-born British photographer. 206
Braque, Georges. (1882-1963) French artist. 262
Brassens, Georges. (1921-1981) French singer-songwriter and poet. 173
Brel, Jacques. (1929-1978) Belgian singer-songwriter and actor. 122
Breton, André. (1896-1966) French writer and poet. 109
Brodovitch, Alexey. (1898-1971) Russian-born American art director. 205
Brooks, David. American cultural commentator. 27
Brouet, Claude. French fashion journalist. 86
Buffon, Georges-Louis Leclerc de. (1707-1778) French naturalist, author and stylist. 48, 49, 214
Burton, Robert. (1577-1640) English scholar and author. 258
Camus, Albert. (1913-1960) French author. 54
Candel, Etienne. French scientific and digital researcher. 167
Capuçon, Renaud. French classical violinist. 238
Caradec, Gaëlle. French journalist. 53
Cardinal de Retz. (1613-1679) French statesman and author. 41
Carlyle, Thomas. (1795-1881) British historian and essayist. 180
Carroll, Lewis. (1832-1898) English author and mathematician. 109, 192, 217
Catinchi, Philippe-Jean. French author and journalist. 257
Céline Louis-Ferdinand. (1894-1961) French novelist and stylist. 122, 171
Chancel, Jacques. (1928-2014) French journalist. 176
Chanel, Coco. (1883-1971) French fashion designer. 49, 242
Chang, Adrien. Hongkong businessman. 67
Char, René. (1907-1988) French poet and resistant. 262
Charles-Roux, Edmonde. (1920-2016) French author. 160

Charpin, Pierre. French designer. 182
Chekhov, Anton. (1860-1904) Russian playwright and short-story writer. 200, 218
Cheng, François. French author. 245
Churchill, Winston. (1874-1965) English statesman. 48, 66, 120, 232, 257
Cicero, Marcus Tullius. (106- 43 B.C.) Roman statesman and scholar. 65
Cieslewicz, Roman. (1930-1996) Polish-born French graphic artist. 190, 192
Claudel, Paul. (1858-1955) French writer. 79
Colette. French concept-store. 9, 56
Collins, Jim. American business researcher and consultant. 130
Comte-Sponville, André. French philosopher. 247
Confucius. (551-479 B.C.) Chinese philosopher. 258
Connes, Alain. French mathematician. 250
Conrad, Joseph. (1857-1924) Polish-British writer. 121
Cotter, Holland. American art critic. 125
Coupland, Douglas. Canadian novelist and artist. 62
Coward, Noël. (1899-1973) English playwright. 122
Crawford, Matthew B. American philosopher and motorcycle mechanic. 109, 235
Cuny, Caroline. French researcher in cognitive psychology. 234
D'Adigné, Marie-Astrid. French student at Penninghen art school. 256
Dahl, Roald. (1916-1990) English author. 76
Da Vinci, Léonardo. (1452-1519) Italian painter and polymath. 199
Dard, Frédéric. (1921-2000) French crime writer. 67
Dassonville, Valérie. Director of the Paris-Villette theatre. 218
Davis, Miles. (1926-1999) American jazz trumpeter. 257
De Botton, Alain. Anglo-suisse philosopher. 131, 243
De Chazal, Malcolm. (1902-1981) Mauritian poet, painter and writer. 225
De Gaulle, Charles. (1890-1970) French statesman. 48, 130
De la Fontaine, Jean. (1621-1695) French fabulist. 122, 186
De La Fouchardière, Tanguy. French business angel. 93
De Lavilleon, Gaëtan. French professor of neuroscience. 235
De Saint Exupéry, Antoine. (1900-1944) French writer and aviator. 154
De Staël, Nicolas. (1914-1955) Russian-French painter. 260
Dehaene, Stanislas. French neuroscientist. 237
Delteil, Joseph. (1894-1978) French poet. 181
Descartes, René. (1629-1649) French philosopher. 120, 172, 175
Devos, Raymond. (1922-2006) Belgian-French humorist. 151
Dickens, Charles. (1812-1870) English author. 120, 182
Diogenes, Laërtius. (3rd century AD) Biographer of Greek philosophers. 229
Dion, Delphine. French marketing professor. 26
Droit, Roger-Pol. French philosopher and author. 54, 66, 168, 192, 229
Drucker, Peter. (1909-2005) Austrian-American business consultant and author. 130
Duarte, Nancy. American communication expert. 233
Durano, Marianne. French philosopher and essayist. 61, 62
Duras, Marguerite. (1914-1996) French novelist and playwright. 263
Dyson, James. English engineer and entrepreneur. 168
Eastwood, Clint. American actor and film director. 238
Echenoz, Jean. French writer. 256
Edmeades, Hugh. British auctioneer. 232
Einfalt, Laurence. French psychologist. 116

Einstein, Albert. (1879-1955) German-Americain theoretical physicist. 116, 198
Elbaz, Alber. (1961-2021) Franco-israeli fashion designer. 54
Eliot, T.S. (1888-1965) American-British poet. 72, 219
Emaz, Antoine. (1955-2019) French poet. 142
Emerson, Ralph Waldo. (1803-1882) American poet and philosopher. 125
English nursery rhyme. 173
Erasmus. (1469-1536) Dutch philosopher and Christian scholar. 137
Evans, Benedict. American digital media analyst. 27
Ferguson, Alex. Scottish football manager. 102
Finlay, Ian Hamilton. (1925-2006) Scottish poet and artist. 119
Fitzgerald, F. Scott. (1896-1940) American author. 258
Flaubert, Gustave. (1821-1880) French novelist. 64, 99, 103, 118, 136, 222, 239
Fletcher, Alan. (1931-2006) British graphic designer. 79, 151, 153, 160, 165, 167, 193, 215, 228, 229, 231
Fontanet, Xavier. French businessman. 238
Ford, Yelena. American-Greek businesswoman. 234
Fourès, Eléna. French executive coach. 93, 233
Fox-Weber, Nicolas. Art historian. 181
France, Anatole. (1844-1924) French author. 239
Franklin, Benjamin. (1706-1790) British-American polymath. 113
Freddo from Irancy. Film technician. 149
Gabart, François. French navigator. 130
Ganesh, Janan. British journalist. 229, 260
Gaston, Pierre-Marc. (1764-1830) French politician and aphorist. 235
Gauguin, Paul. (1848-1903) French painter. 186, 193
Gaultier, Jean-Paul. French fashion designer. 86
Gauthier, Marie-Bénédicte. French beauty expert. 40
Gautier, Théophile. (1811-1872) French author. 257
Gerald, Casey. American writer. 257
Gerber, Michael E. American business consultant and author. 26, 93
Germond, Michel. French cabinet-maker teacher. 236
Gide, André. (1869-1951) French author. 155, 256
Gigerenzer, Gerd. German psychologist. 136
Gladwell, Malcolm. Canadian author. 184
Goethe, Johann Wolfgang von. (1749-1832) German writer. 254, 255
Gowers, Ernest. (1880-1966) English language stylist. 200
Graves, Robert. (1895-1985) British poet and author. 214
Green, Eugène. American film maker. 65
Grozdanovitch, Denis. French author. 37
Guidi, Guido. Italian photographer. 180
Guillem, Sylvie. French ballet dancer. 200
Guitton, Jean. (1901-1999) French Catholic philosopher. 67, 72, 73, 79, 87, 121, 122, 143, 215, 216, 224, 230, 235, 236, 239
Gursky, Andreas. German photographer. 223
Hamilton, William.L. American Rabbi. 147
Harford, Tim. English undercover economist and journalist. 93, 121, 174, 207
Hatchuel, Armand. French professor of management sciences. 250
Heathcote, Edwin. English architect. 201, 224
Hegarty, John. English advertising mogul. 26, 125, 150, 170, 197, 200
Hegel, Georg Wilhelm Friedrich. (1770-1831) German philosopher. 64

Heidegger, Martin. (1889-1976) German philosopher. 200
Henno, Jacques. French specialist in information technologies. 34
Heraclitus. (535-475 BC)Ancient Greek philosopher. 260
Hiro. Japanese-born American photographer. 78, 173
Hockney, David. English artist. 98
Hoffmann-Feet, Alfred. Swiss typographer. 55
Holtzman, Jean. Perfume executive. 131
Hong, Euny. Korean author. 131
Horace. (65-27 BC) Roman lyric poet. 122
Hugo, Victor. (1802-1885) French author. 40
Igarashi, Takenobu. Japanese graphic designer. 181
Irving, John. American-Canadian novelist. 40
Ïto, Ora. French designer. 198
Ive, Jonathan. English designer. 39
Jabès, Edmond. (1912-1991) French poet of Egyptian origin. 37
Jackson, Will. English robot constructor. 166
Jacobs, Emma. English journalist. 26
James, Henry. (1843-1916) American-British author. 7
Jaurès, Jean. French politician. 238
Jensen, Jacob. (1926-2015) Danish industrial designer. 79
Jobs, Steve. (1955-2011) American business magnate. 109, 131, 136, 171, 250
Jodelet, René. French blacksmith. 176, 177
Johnson, Steven Berlin. American writer. 144, 149
Jones, Eddie. Australian Rugby coach. 133
Joubert, Joseph. (1754-1824) French thinker. 49, 102, 124, 127, 149, 160, 172, 194, 198, 199, 216, 217, 218, 219, 224, 228, 237, 242, 243
Judd, Donald. (1928-1994) American artist. 69, 200
Judor, Eric. French actor. 26
Keats, John. (1795-1821) English poet. 48, 245, 247
Kennedy, Pagan. American columnist. 36
Kervern, Alain. French haïku author. 186
Kessels, Erik. Dutch artist and curator. 251
Kiefer, Anselm. German painter. 170
Kierkegaard. (1813-1855) Danish philosopher. 169
Klee, Paul. (1879-1940) Swiss-German painter. 79
Klopp, Jürgen. German football coach. 122
Knight, India. British journalist. 62
Knight, Nick. English photographer. 155, 204, 207
Koolhaas, Rem. Dutch architect. 263
Kuper, Simon. British author. 238
Lagerfeld, Karl. German fashion designer. 65, 120, 152, 167, 207, 254, 257
Lartigue, Jacques-Henri. (1894-1986) French photographer. 204
Lavant, Denis. French actor. 175
Le Bon, Laurent. French art historian. 113
Le Corbusier. (1887-1965) Swiss-French architect. 112, 118
Leith, Sam. English author. 233
Lejeune, Antoine. French neurologist. 73
Lewis, Sarah. American art historian. 125
Leys, Simon. (1935-2014) Belgian-Australian writer. 228
Lichtenstein, Roy. (1923-1997) American artist. 86

Lismore, Daniel. British fabric designer. 153, 254
Lledo, Pierre-Marie. French neuroscientist. 234
Lloyd, Christopher. (1921-2006) English gardener and writer. 40
London, Jack. (1876-1916) American journalist. 103
Luckey, Palmer. American entrepreneur. 151
Lüpertz, Markus. German artist. 175
Luti, Claudio. Italian businessman. 73
Lynch, David. American artist and film director. 37, 149
MacDonald, Hugo. English design journalist. 117
Madoz, Chema. Spanish photographer. 149
Maeda, John. American designer and professor. 196
Magretta, Joan. American business professor. 132
Maldini, Paolo. Italian footballer. 38
Mandela, Nelson. (1918-2015) South African statesman. 236
Manguel, Alberto. Argentine-Canadian writer. 142, 144, 224
Mansau, Serge. (1930-2019) French perfume bottle designer. 254
Marlowe, Christopher. (1564-1593) English playwright. 244
Martin, Pia. French communication coach. 232
Martinez, Virgilio. Peruvian chef. 260
Maugham, Somerset. (1874-1965) English author. 145
McCandless, David. British data-journalist. 238
McQueen, Alexander. English fashion designer. 263
McQueen, Steve. British artist. 247
Mélanchon, Jean-Luc. French politician. 117
Michel, Philippe. (1940- 1993) French adman. 149
Milne, A.A. (1882-1956) English author. 117
Mishakova, Olena. Ukranian recruitment expert. 128
Molga, Paul. French journalist. 133
Moncler. : French fashion brand. 257
Monet, Claude. (1840-1926) French painter. 99, 193
Monk, Thelonious. (1917-1982) American jazz pianist. 257
Montaigne, Michel de. (1533-1592) French philosopher.
7, 169, 184, 223, 227, 229, 239, 258
Montesquieu. (1689-1755) French thinker. 133
Moon, Sarah. French photographer. 78
Morandi, Giorgio. (1890-1964) Italian painter. 181
Munch, Edvard. (1863-1944) Norwegian painter. 34, 36
Nabokov, Vladimir. (1899-1977) Russian-American novelist. 219
Nadar, [aka Gaspard-Félix Tournachon] (1820-1910) French photographer.
199, 181, 248
Nayar, Vineet. Indian business executive. 132
Nelson, Horatio. (1758-1805) British flag officer. 127
Newton, Isaac. (1643-1727) English scientist. 32, 33
Nietzsche, Friedrich. (1844-1900) German philosopher. 173, 258
Noiville, Florence. French writer. 174, 251
Norman, Jessye. (1945-2019) American opera singer. 254
Norris, Rufus. British theatre director. 66
Nouvel, Jean. French architect. 152, 188, 205, 250
O'Keefe, Georgia. (1887-1986) American artist. 257
O'Leary, Michael. Irish businessman. 200

O'Neil, Baroness. British philosopher. 130
Ollman, Arthur. American photographer. 36
Onesta, Claude. French handball coach. 133
Orwell, George. (1903-1950) English author. 34, 35, 172, 215, 222, 227
Palin, Michael. English actor. Cf Monty Python. 118
Pamuk, Orhan. Turkish novelist. 72
Pang, Alex Soojung-Kim. Silicon Valley consultant. 169
Pascal, Blaise. (1623-1662) French religious philosopher. 86, 242
Pasteur, Louis. (1822-1895) French microbiologist. 37
Pawson, John. English architect. 88, 200
Payot, Jules. (1859-1940) French educationist. 121
Pearce, Harry. English graphic designer. 247
Peascod, Emma. English designer. 244
Pechère, René. (1908-2002) Belgian landscape gardener. 160, 244
Penn, Irving. (1917-2009) American photographer. 89, 175, 178, 181, 205, 208, 227
Penninghen students. 37, 251, 256, 271
Perec, Georges. (1936-1982) French author. 111, 262
Perriand, Charlotte. (1903-1999) French architect. 167, 182
Perucca, Brigitte. French journalist. 169
Pessoa, Fernando. (1888-1935) Portugese author. 77, 180, 181, 215, 238
Péters, Sophie. French business coach. 199
Petillon, Monique. French journalist. 142
Phelan, Hayley. Canadian writer. 143
Piano, Renzo. Italian architect. 155, 243
Picasso, Pablo. (1881-1993) Spanish painter. 49, 78, 170, 248
Piguet, Philippe. French art historian. 198
Plautus. (254-184 BC) Roman playwright. 55
Plutarch. (46-125) Greek philosopher. 238
Pop, Iggy. American musician. 200
Poswick, Phyllis. American fashion journalist. 175
Potet, Frédéric. French journalist. 225
Powell, Gary. Film stunt co-ordinator. 247
Proust, Marcel. (1871-1922) French novelist. 49, 64, 69, 137, 140, 185
Puchner, Martin. German philosopher. 224
Rabanne, Paco. Spanish fashion designer. 38, 169
Rams, Dieter. German industrial designer. 200
Rancinan, Gérard. French photographer. 78
Rao, Mahesh. Author. 61
Reps, Paul. (1895-1990) American poet. 180
Richards, Blake. Canadian cognitive scientist. 73
Ridel, Stéphane. French film maker. 160
Rivierre, Adrien. French communications expert. 233
Robert, Martine. French journalist. 67
Roberts, Anabelle. French communications expert. 233
Robinson, Ken. (1950-2020) English educationist. 99
Rock, Michael. American graphic designer. 77
Rookledge, Gavin. English bookbinder. 142
Rosling, Hans. (1948-2017) Swedish statistician. 65
Rosset, Clément. (1939-2018) French philosopher. 215
Roth, Philip. (1933-2018) American novelist. 251

Rousseau, Yann. French journalist. 78
Roy, Nilanjana. Indian journalist. 62, 225
Rubright, Linda. American author. 171
Saglio, Philippe. French art director. 245
Saint Augustine. (354-430) Roman theologian. 193
Saint Laurent, Yves. (1936-2008) French fashion designer. 117, 180
Santi, Jean-Guillaume. French journalist. 103
Sartre, Jean-Paul. (1905-1980) French philosopher. 257
Savignac, Raymond. (1907-2002) French graphic artist. 200
Saville, Peter. English graphic designer. 144, 198
Sax, David. Canadian journalist. 63
Scarry, Olympia. Swiss artist. 112
Schmitt, Eric-Emmanuel. Franco-Belgian writer. 152
Sempé, Jean-Jacques. (1932-2022) French cartoonist. 121
Serres, Michel. (1930-2019) French philosopher. 22
Sertillanges, Antonin-Gilbert. (1863-1948) French catholic philosopher. 153, 155
Shakespeare, William. (1564-1616) English playwright. 41, 120, 158
Sheldrake, Christopher. English perfumer. 260
Shepard, Sam. (1943-2017) American actor and director. 62
Simon, Claude. (1913-2005) French novelist. 219
Simone, Nina. (1933-2003) American singer-songwriter. 41
Smith, Kiki. American artist. 167
Smith, Paul. English fashion designer. 37
Socrates. (470-399 B.C.) Greek philosopher. 7, 239
Solotareff, Grégoire. French artist and illustrator. 117
Soloviev, Vladimir. (1853-1900) Russian philosopher. 242
Sotto, Alain. French educational psychologist. 73
Soulages, Pierre. French artist. 79
Starck, Philippe. French designer. 165, 178, 238
Swift, Jonathan. (1667-1745) Anglo-Irish satirist. 49
Swinburne, Algernon Charles. (1837-1909) English poet. 126
Systrom, Kevin. American computer programmer. 257
Talbot, Caroline. French journalist. 234
Taleb, Nassim Nicolas. Lebanese-American essayist. 117
Tavoillot, Paul-André. French communication expert. 232
Tavoillot, Pierre-Henri. French philosopher. 66
Terrail, Claude. (1917-2006) Restaurateur. 125
Terzieff, Laurent. (1935-2010) French actor. 37
Tesson, Sylvain. French writer. 61, 229, 242, 250
Therin, Frédéric. French journalist. 77
Thomas, Henri. (1912-1993) French writer. 112
Tillmans, Wolfgang. German photographer. 208
Tyson, Mike. American boxer. 109
Valéry, Paul. (1871-1945) French author. 49, 185, 198, 217, 228
Vanden Berghen, Christian. Belgian business consultant. 33
Vanderbilt, Tom. American journalist. 112
Vanier, Nicolas. French adventurist. 133
Verdier, Fabienne. French calligrapher. 103, 262
Vorpsi, Ornela. Albanian writer. 185
Walker, Tim. English photographer. 246, 247

Wall, Jeff. Canadian photographer. 205, 207
Walpole, Horace. (1717-1797) English writer. 31
Waters, Richard. English journalist. 41
Watterson, Bill. American cartoonist. 39
WeiWei, Ai. Chinese artist. 155
Whale, John. (1931-2008) English journalist. 214, 216
Wilde, Oscar. (1854-1900) Irish poet. 151, 229, 244, 255
Williams, Robbie. English singer-songwriter. 103
Willingham, Daniel T. American psychologist. 62
Wilson, Edward Osborne. American biologist. 137
Wols. [aka **Alfred Otto Wolfgang Schulze**]. (1913-1951) German painter. 182
Woolf, Virginia. (1882-1941) English writer. 223
Wullschläger, Jackie. English art critic. 78
Zola, Emile. (1840-1902) French novelist. 137

BRANDS

Amazon. 50, 92, 110
Apple. 27, 39, 103, 164, 196
Aston Martin. 44
Cadbury. 44
Carlsberg. 44
Clarins. 7, 157, 215
Coca-Cola. 44
Colette. 7, 56
Dior. 55, 164
Facebook. 44
Ferrari. 44, 46
Galeries Lafayette. 59
Givaudan. 7, 38, 138, 139, 157
Google. 52, 61, 62, 65, 110
Hermès. 44, 236, 255
L'Oréal. 7, 65, 138, 139, 236
Lancôme. 7, 44, 56, 59, 155, 157, 176, 208

Lexus. 78
Louis Vuitton. 84, 147
LVMH. 109, 197
Mark & Spencer. 43
McDonald's. 106
Microsoft. 61
Nestlé. 39, 45
Nike. 59
Orange. 51, 52
Paco Rabanne. 38, 169
Romanée Conti. 76, 85
Royal Bank of Scotland. 50
Selfridges. 44
Silk Cut. 44
Tiffany. 44, 45
Toyota. 78
Weston. 236

Almost all the French quotations were translated into English by the author.

Scanners finders; finders keepers.

MOST STEPS WINS

A BRAND IS AN ONION
was printed in France using
environmentally friendly techniques: the
dampening solution, photographic plates,
photographic development products,
scraps of paper and inks were recycled
after use.

Printed in June 2023 by Escourbiac
(Graulhet, France)
ISBN: 978-2-909478-61-6
Dépôt légal : mai 2023